Tim and Erik and their company, Corporate Visions, have devoted the last several years to conducting some of the most rigorous studies ever done on B2B selling, and they've uncovered some compelling insights into precisely what's different about the selling motion for an existing customer versus an acquisition prospect. In this book, they turn those insights into tactics that every company should build into their customer engagement and expansion plans.

—NICK MEHTA, CEO of Gainsight
and author of *Customer Success*

When looking to accelerate growth, companies tend to focus on net new acquisitions, ignoring the unmined gold they already have in their current customer base. This book provides sales, marketing, and customer service leaders a tested, proven, and practical approach for tapping into this deep vein of potential revenue.

—TIFFANI BOVA, Customer Growth and
Innovation Evangelist at Salesforce and
bestselling author of *Growth IQ*

This book is critical for anyone in a B2B organization who interacts with existing customers. The research shows there is a distinct difference in the way marketing and sales must communicate with existing customers in critical buying conversations.

—DR. NICK LEE, Professor of Marketing, Warwick Business School, and Corporate Visions Research Partner

The Expansion Sale by Corporate Visions will be a must-read for strategic and key account managers. Expanding the business relationship is their most significant role . . . across all client levels and departments! These four conversations are a fundamental part of an account manager's everyday responsibilities.

—DENISE FREIER, President and CEO, Strategic Account Management Association (SAMA)

This groundbreaking book details original research around how to optimize existing customer messaging in a variety of familiar situations that have received surprisingly little attention in the past. Importantly, the book translates these studies into practical guidance for executives seeking to drive more growth from existing customers.

—NICK DE CENT, Editor in Chief, *The International Journal of Sales Transformation*

THE
EXPANSION
>SALE<

THE
EXPANSION
SALE

Four Must-Win Conversations to Keep and Grow Your Customers

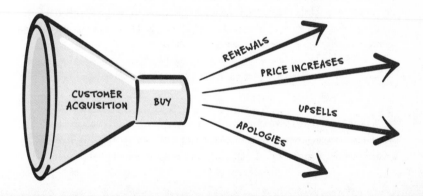

ERIK PETERSON • TIM RIESTERER

In Collaboration with DR. NICK LEE

ROB PERRILLEON • JOE COLLINS • DOUG HUTTON • LESLIE TALBOT

Mc
Graw
Hill

NEW YORK   CHICAGO   SAN FRANCISCO   ATHENS   LONDON
MADRID   MEXICO CITY   MILAN   NEW DELHI
SINGAPORE   SYDNEY   TORONTO

1 2 3 4 5 6 7 8 9   LCR   25 24 23 22 21 20

ISBN   978-1-260-46275-3
MHID   1-260-46275-7

e-ISBN   978-1-260-46276-0
e-MHID   1-260-46276-5

Design by Lee Fukui and Mauna Eichner

This publication is designed to provide accurate and authoritative information in regard to the subject matter covered. It is sold with the understanding that neither the author nor the publisher is engaged in rendering legal, accounting, securities trading, or other professional services. If legal advice or other expert assistance is required, the services of a competent professional person should be sought.
   —*From a Declaration of Principles Jointly Adopted by a Committee of the American Bar Association and a Committee of Publishers and Associations*

McGraw-Hill Education books are available at special quantity discounts to use as premiums and sales promotions or for use in corporate training programs. To contact a representative, please visit the Contact Us pages at www.mhprofessional.com.

Contents

Research Note   vii

Foreword
Nick Mehta, Chief Executive Officer, Gainsight   ix

Acknowledgments   xi

Introduction   xv

PART I

DEVELOPING THE EXPANSION MESSAGE

1 Acquisition Does Not Equal Expansion   5

2 Expansion Messaging—Mission Critical,
   but Missing in Action   25

3 Why Stay and the Psychology Behind Renewals   35

4 Cracking the Code on the
   Price Increase Conversation   47

5 Why Pay More—A Framework for Improving
   Your Price Increase Conversations   57

6 Messaging for the Upsell—The Why Evolve
   Conversation   69

7   The Winning Why Evolve Message Framework   75

8   "Sorry" Shouldn't Be the Hardest Word—
    Apology Science and the Expansion Sale   89

9   The Winning Why Forgive Message Framework   99

PART II
DELIVERING THE EXPANSION MESSAGE

10 The Right Message at the Right Time—Mastering
    Situational Fluency   121

11 Delivering the Message—Essential Skills
    for the Expansion Seller   135

12 Navigating the Conversation—Advanced Skills
    for the Expansion Seller   159

13 Expansion Messaging as a Commercial Strategy   177

14 Parting Thoughts   191

    Appendix: Real-World Examples   195

    Index   213

    About the Authors   227

Research Note

One thing that's always struck us about much academic research is that it's, well, *academic*. Researchers tend to study the most readily available subjects, which tend to be graduate students, gamblers, and convicts. While that might be great for getting access to a captive audience (no pun intended), we had to wonder how "real world" the results really are. What's the use of doing B2B research if you're not tapping a B2B research subject pool?

That's why, throughout this book, you'll see that our study results report on simulations conducted with actual business-people, including executive buyers. You know, the people you actually want to become your customers!

In addition, we're very much proponents of Decision Science. There's a lot that's been written about the "best-practices" approach to research. But that means you're starting with a built-in bias around what the "right" answer is. One thing we have learned from our research is that the right answer is often the most counterintuitive answer. Starting with an ideal of what a best practice is will skew that perspective.

Best practices also are inherently "lagging practices." It can take years to identify something as a best practice, and by that time, it's a common practice. Best practices also suffer from being inherently company-centric and regional. Decision

Science, on the other hand, is completely focused on the buyers and their behavior. And it's also timeless and globally applicable.

Finally, although you see we do use some industry surveys in our research, we don't rely on those surveys to generate results. For us, surveys are simply one window into the customer's current thinking. In fact, one thing we know is that there's often a gap between what people say they believe ("declared preferences") and what they actually do ("revealed preferences"). Within that gap is where some of our most startling, counterintuitive results originate—and that's what our scientific simulations aim to uncover.

Of course, we owe a tremendous debt of gratitude to our research partners, Dr. Nick Lee, a coauthor of this book, and Dr. Zakary Tormala, who participated in some of the early research studies around retention and renewal:

- **Dr. Nick Lee** is Professor of Marketing at Warwick Business School in Coventry, UK. He has spent nearly 20 years drawing from social psychology, cognitive neuroscience, economics, and philosophy to develop insights into salespeople and selling.

- **Dr. Zakary Tormala** is a social psychologist with expertise in the areas of messaging and persuasion. He was contracted by Corporate Visions to create this research, conduct the experiments, and help ensure academic rigor and empirically valid results. Dr. Tormala is a professor at the Stanford Graduate School of Business.

Foreword

For buyers, the subscription economy promised manageable prices for instant value. Prohibitively costly goods could be had immediately for lower recurring payments. The barriers to entry and exit were lower, so buyers were no longer locked into bad deals by huge investments.

But what about the promise this bargain made to vendors? As long as you were meeting the customers' needs, the lifetime value of the relationship could grow—infinitely, in theory—and customers would renew automatically, forever.

However, I recently heard a poignant quote from a head of sales: "In a competitive market, renewals are really resells."

That's a troubling premise for recurring revenue businesses. If renewals are no longer automatic, that means the renewal conversation is suddenly a critical moment in every customer relationship.

And that's where this incredible book comes in. It makes a compelling case that renewals are resells, but it goes further to show that the sales motion you used to close the acquisition sale is not the sales motion you should use to close the expansion sale. Just as the subscription economy demanded changes in your support model, your financial model, and your product development model, it also needs to drive a change in your selling model.

Erik and Tim and their company, Corporate Visions, have devoted the last several years to conducting some of the most rigorous studies ever done on B2B selling, and they've uncovered some compelling insights into precisely what's different about the selling motion for an existing customer versus an acquisition prospect. In this book, they turn those insights into tactics that every company should build into their customer engagement and expansion plans.

But speaking as a geek for all things scientific, my favorite part of the book is all the fascinating insight into buying and selling psychology. I hope you'll find it as captivating as I did!

Nick Mehta
Chief Executive Officer
Gainsight

Acknowledgments

Erik Peterson

Everything good in my life flows from the fact that my wife, Christie, accepted my proposal more than 25 years ago. When I was faced with two career paths—one that meant more income and less travel, and the other that brought me to Corporate Visions—Christie urged me to take the Corporate Visions job because she knew I would love it. She was right, as I have come to expect, and I have been blessed to do this work ever since. We are also blessed with three wonderful boys, Jeremy, Zachary, and Brett, whom I could brag about for thousands of words. But that would be another book. Suffice it to say that I do this work in the hope that they can see some of the results (like this book) and be as proud of their dad as I am of them.

Tim Riesterer

To all the women in my life: Laura, my love, you make this world a better place for everyone you meet, and make me a better man; Rachel, Emily, Anna, and Hope, you've grown up to be amazing young women with caring hearts, just like your mother; Little Rosie, thank you for your precious smile and sweet spirit, which helps me accept the reality that I'm old enough to be a grandpa. Mom, your positive spirit and gift of encouragement is as meaningful now as it was 50 years ago. Mary and Dad, thank you for your constant love, presence, and support for all we do. Kia, my goddaughter, and her family, thank you for increasing our family's capacity to love and be loved. To God be the glory!

Nick Lee

I would like to thank in particular Tim, Erik, and everyone else at Corporate Visions for their enthusiasm and interest. It's been a real pleasure and an education working with them on these and all our other studies over the last few years. I'd especially like to thank Tim for giving me the opportunity to be a part of what is a really fun double act in presenting this work too and making it all seem so easy! Of course, as always, I'd like to thank my wonderfully supportive wife, Laura, who always helps me see the good in things and encourages me always to take the opportunity to do interesting and fun stuff, like this!

Rob Perrilleon

Thank you to my wife, Jessica, who not only supported but encouraged my career change to Corporate Visions. Like so many other times, you knew what would make me happy better than I did. And thank you for the countless times and ways you have supported me since. Thank you to my sons, Justin and

Evan, for being a constant reminder of what really matters in life. Seeing the character and maturity you have developed lets me sleep soundly at night, even when too many of those early nights were away from home. Thank you to Erik and Tim for your leadership, vision, and trust and for making CVI unlike any other place to work. Thank you to the consulting team and all my great colleagues at CVI. "Inspired" is an overused term, but I can think of nothing better to describe the incredibly high standard you set. Finally, thank you to the great mentors I had early in my career: Mark, Erik, Tom, Todd, Greg, Jim.

Joe Collins

If you believe that life is a journey, then it really matters whom you walk with. For over 20 years, I could not have asked for a better partner than my wife, Tracie. She is the nucleus of our family and my best friend, and she enables us all to strive for more. Thank you for everything you do! To my kids, Joseph and Lillian, you are amazing. As a parent, over half the time I have no idea what I am doing, and yet despite that, you kids have grown into interesting, intelligent, and entertaining teenagers. I can't wait to see what paths you take as adults. I'd also like to thank my parents and my sisters. As I was growing up, they provided the perfect amount of fun, support, craziness, and love. Each one of them helped me find my path, and I am grateful to you all. For all my friends and family that I couldn't mention, just know that you are loved and appreciated.

Doug Hutton

I'd like to thank my wife, Cassandra, for her patience and grace at home while I'm earning too many award miles visiting our clients. To my children, Addison and Carter, for often being the guinea pigs as I try out new whiteboards and practice client messages. To all my coauthors, for continually pushing my thinking and disrupting my own Status Quo Bias. And as the aspiring pilot of the group, to my flight instructor, Hunter Driscoll. He never knew what he was getting into when he accepted that first request.

Leslie Talbot

I was fortunate to have been born into the most wonderful family anyone could hope for. To my dad, for his wisdom and resilience—you have always pushed me to be the best I can be, and I am eternally grateful for that. To my sisters, Liz and Leigh, for their lifelong love and support—you are truly my best and closest friends. To my mom, for your brilliance and determination—I miss you every day. Thank you also to my mentors Erik and Tim, my coauthors, and to the CVI Content team—particularly Leif Kothe, Brent Alwood, Michelina Jones, Justin Barry, and Jessica Zimmerman—who brought these ideas to brilliant life with their words and art. It's a privilege to work with you all.

Introduction

As a native Midwesterner, one of our authors, Tim, grew up with an unhealthy phobia of tornadoes. Thankfully, his town had the foresight to install a siren warning system that would alert the populace—all 600 souls—to a looming threat should the occasion arise.

The town tested the siren every day at noon, sounding a minute-long ear-shattering blast, rain or shine. Yet somehow the townspeople managed to ignore the piercing wail and go about their business, a few fondly referring to it as the "noon whistle."

Then one memorable day, the skies darkened. The clouds began to rumble. And the siren went off at 3 p.m. This was it. The real deal! And 13 panicked teenagers who had been playing ball in the park sprang into action. Instead of ignoring the siren, the kids jumped on their bikes and pedaled as fast as they could to get home to the safety of their basements (more than a few crying for their mommies, according to a reliable eyewitness).

Thankfully, no tornado touched down in that little town that afternoon, and none have officially touched down in its entire 200-year history. But in that frantic moment, a lesson in marketing, sales, and customer service was born.

Turns out, it wasn't about the siren at all. It was about the context of the situation the siren was in.

It's a phenomenon called the Context Effect. As illustrated in Figure I.1, the Context Effect is *the influence of environmental factors on the perception of a stimulus*. No one cared about the screeching siren when it was doing its thing at noon every day. But when the situation changed to threatening, everyone cared. And responded accordingly.

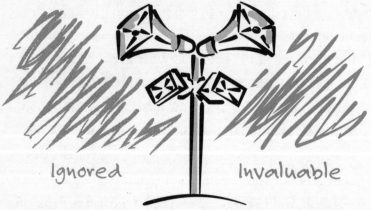

Context Effect

Influence of environmental factors on the perception of a stimulus

Ignored   Invaluable

Figure I.1 Are you ignored or invaluable? Context matters.

It was the different environment that made the siren irrelevant one minute and invaluable the next. It had nothing to do with the tensile strength of the horn or the decibel levels it put out.

The Context Effect is essential to marketing, selling, and customer success as well. It's not your products or services that get people to respond. It's their environmental factors, their current situation, that determine their perception of your solution.

Chief among these environmental factors is whether they are a prospect doing something else with someone else (or perhaps doing nothing at all with anyone) or whether they are your existing customer doing that thing with you.

The Context Effect calls for you to develop and deliver a message differently to prospects versus existing customers. After all, their environment is very different when it comes to responding to your stimulus . . . er, your products and services.

Wait! You say you don't message differently or you're unsure of the distinction. Then you've come to the right place. This book is for you. And it will completely change your perspective on—and approach to—marketing, sales, and customer success.

Inside, you'll find brand-new, exclusive research on the difference between customer acquisition and customer expansion messaging. While many books have been written about how to get new customers, this is the first to show you how to *keep and grow* the customers you already have.

After all, according to many analysts your existing customers represent 70–80 percent of your revenue and growth opportunities. So it's critical you get these customer conversations right. Yet most companies take the same one-size-fits-all approach to marketing, sales, and customer success when renewing and upselling existing customers as they did to acquire them in the first place.

Recent research proves this will backfire—badly. In fact, the psychology of the existing customer is 180 degrees different from the psychology of a prospect. That means the stories and skills you use to communicate with them need to be 180 degrees different as well.

FOUR MUST-WIN COMMERCIAL MOMENTS

There are several things you must do after winning a new customer that are vital to the customer's experience and satisfaction, including onboarding, change management, adoption, and utilization, not to mention ensuring your customer achieves the results you promised. While these are important, this book doesn't focus on these day-to-day customer success activities.

Instead, it focuses entirely on the four must-win commercial moments in every customer relationship:

1. Renewals

2. Price increases

3. Upsells

4. Apologies

These are the acute scenarios in which you rally your organization's marketing, sales, and customer success resources to keep and grow your customers. They're also the tense situations that register highest on the revenue "Richter Scale," where much of your (and your company's) success hangs in the balance.

It's in these moments you need tested, proven customer conversation message frameworks and skills, rooted in decision-making science and the invisible forces that shape how people frame value and make choices.

And that's what you'll get in this book: specific, practical, actionable approaches to create and deliver your message for maximum impact in these make-or-break moments.

THE
EXPANSION
≥SALE≤

PART I

DEVELOPING THE EXPANSION MESSAGE

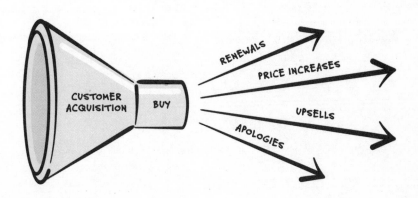

In this section, you'll learn the brain science behind developing effective communications for the four must-win commercial moments in customer expansion: getting your customers to renew with you (Why Stay); asking them to accept a price increase and stick with you (Why Pay More); convincing them to upgrade or buy more from you (Why Evolve); and getting them to accept your apology for a service problem (Why Forgive).

Whether you're a marketer, a seller, or a customer success professional, these must-win customer conversations all too often happen by accident rather than on purpose. But if you follow the frameworks in the following chapters, you will be able to build messages that have been tested and proven to increase your chances of keeping and growing your existing customers.

1

Acquisition Does Not Equal Expansion

Sometimes we joke that people get into marketing, sales, or customer success to avoid science and math. Yet it turns out you need a lot of science (and, sadly, quite a bit of math) to truly understand how to influence people's buying decisions.

There's even an entire area of study devoted to the topic. It's called "Decision Science," and it explores the invisible forces that shape how human beings frame value and make choices. If you've read our previous books, *Conversations That Win the Complex Sale* and *The Three Value Conversations*, you learned how to use the power of neuroscience, social psychology, and behavioral economics to convince prospects to change and choose you. In this book, you're going to see how you can harness those same hidden forces to convince prospects to expand their existing business with you.

But this time there's a twist.

The principles of Decision Science still apply to renewal and expansion conversations. But new research conducted with our partners, Dr. Zakary Tormala and Dr. Nick Lee, proves that you need to approach these conversations in a radically different way.

This revelation will likely surprise everyone who's bought into the hype around "provocation-based selling" that has dominated sales and marketing over the past decade. It certainly surprised us.

However, when we stepped back and reexamined the science, it made perfect sense.

STATUS QUO BIAS—DISRUPT OR DEFEND?

It all starts with a scientifically proven decision-making concept called "Status Quo Bias." In our previous books, we shared the four reasons why people don't change their minds—why they prefer to stick with their status quo.

Our research showed that you need to disrupt and defeat Status Quo Bias when you are attempting to poach a prospect from a competitor or do-it-yourselfer. However, our newest studies demonstrated that you must actually defend and reinforce Status Quo Bias when you are, well, the status quo.

That's because prospects and customers are answering different questions in their mind. The *prospects* want to know why they need to change and do something different, and why they need to do it now, not later. Meanwhile, your *existing customers* are asking themselves different questions. They are trying to determine why they should stay with you, and possibly buy more from you.

In each environment the factors ("Context Effect") are different. Meaning the psychology of your audience is different. The questions you must answer are different. That means the resulting stories and skills must be different (Figure 1.1).

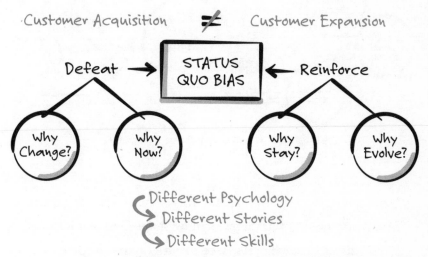

Figure 1.1 Different context (customer psychology) requires different stories and different skills.

As reinforcement for those of you who read our previous books, and in preparation for those of you who are new to our work, here's a quick refresher on Status Quo Bias and how you must disrupt it to answer the "Why Change" question for a prospect (Figure 1.2).

In his paper *The Psychology of Doing Nothing*, research psychologist Christopher J. Anderson detailed four causes, or "antecedents," of Status Quo Bias: "Preference Stability," "Perceived Cost of Change," "Selection Difficulty," and

Status Quo Bias

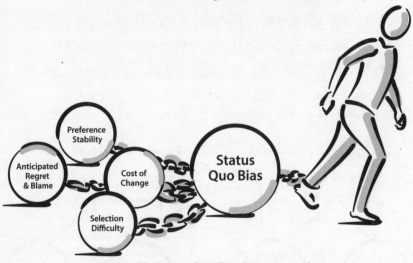

Figure 1.2 Status Quo Bias keeps people chained to their current state.

"Anticipated Regret and Blame."* This is a useful starting point for anyone looking to understand how Status Quo Bias informs buying decisions, when it's necessary to disrupt or defend it, and—most importantly—how to do so.

1. **Preference Stability.** People naturally dislike uncertainty. They made previous decisions that became their preferences. As a result, any new information that threatens those preferences and their stability must be resolved quickly. The typical

---

* Christopher Anderson, "The Psychology of Doing Nothing: Forms of Decision Avoidance Result from Reason and Emotion," *Psychological Bulletin*, 129 (2003): 139–167. 10.1037//0033-2909.129.1.139.

words you may hear when a prospect is reestablishing Preference Stability are such comments as "This seems a lot like the way I'm already doing it." Or "This seems a lot like what everyone else is saying."

Hearing the word "like" might be a good thing in social media posts, but it's a problem in selling. Introducing uncertainty about your prospects' status quo is a prerequisite for change, but their natural reaction will be to avoid it, push back, and try to resolve it in their minds.

Even though they accept that their current approach might not be perfect, they will rationalize that it isn't bad enough to take on the risk of a big change management project.

2. **Perceived Cost of Change.** Your prospects see their status quo as free. It's viewed as just part of their operating budget and internal operating rhythm or cadence. They don't have to think about it too much. If they were to consider a change, your prospects imagine all the new costs they might encounter.

Additional budget money may be needed to pay for the start-up costs that they already paid when they purchased the existing solution. Furthermore, there are the added costs associated with onboarding, training, and process changes required to accommodate any solution change-out. And then factor in the time and effort required to build consensus among all the decision makers and users.

Making the change looks like it will cost them money, time, and stomach lining. Again, while the existing approach may not be perfect, they think doing that new thing with that new provider is a hard, risky change management project not worth this added cost to them or their company.

3. **Selection Difficulty.** The amount of information your prospect must sift through and process to make a buying decision is overwhelming. Most marketers and sellers don't help this situation when they keep piling on the messaging and content during a selling process. At some point the prospect shuts down and declares all providers the same, essentially shutting down the deal at the same time.

   The decision-making part of the brain is very simple and doesn't even contain the capacity for language. What it needs, and what it's looking for, is clear contrast between what people are already doing today and what you are recommending. People won't make a decision to change if they think they are getting something similar to their current approach.

   Their thought process goes like this: "Change is so risky and costly, why would I go through all that just to get something that is more or less the same as what I already have?"

4. **Anticipated Regret and Blame.** The fourth cause of Status Quo Bias is very insidious. Deep down, your prospects may know their current approach isn't

perfect and even agree that on paper, your solution is better. But they worry about what will happen if the change doesn't go well.

The subconscious thinking goes this way: "What we're doing today isn't perfect, but hey, at least I'm not dead yet! That change management project you are proposing and I'm sponsoring . . . that thing could kill me."

Of course, they don't mean this literally, but the brain's natural survival mechanism kicks in at some point in the process and assesses the risk of making the change compared with the pains of staying the same. And the very real pressure of risk aversion threatens to stop all your progress.

The Myth of the Emotionless Executive

There's a widespread assumption that seasoned business executives are rational decision makers. They assess risks and weigh rewards with a keen, calculating eye and make coldly logical choices based on hard numbers. They might use different criteria when weighing a personal decision, or so the thinking goes, but when it comes to business, it's "just the facts, ma'am."

We wondered how valid those assumptions are. After all, executives are human beings. Don't their brains follow the same scientific rules as everyone else's?

Since "selling to the C-suite" is near the top of all our clients' wish lists, we decided to study how emotion, specifically humans' natural loss aversion, affects decisions made at the highest level of an organization.

In partnership with Dr. Zakary Tormala, we constructed a research study with 113 executives from a cross section of industries around the world. We asked the executives to each imagine that they were an auto manufacturing executive whose business was experiencing hard times and needed to make a difficult decision about closing plants and eliminating jobs. With their current status quo, there was a risk of needing to close up to three plants and losing up to 6,000 jobs. While each executive had that same starting point, from there the executives were split into two groups. Both groups would hear very similar options for what they might do to improve the plant and job situation, but the options would be framed differently depending on which group the executive was in.

One group would have its status quo presented in a "gain" frame, and one group would have its status quo presented in a "loss" frame. We'll show you how those frames were worded, so you can see what was different between the two.

The first group was told it had two options. Plan A would save one out of three plants and 2,000 jobs. Plan B was a riskier option. Plan B gave the executives a 33 percent chance of saving all three plants and 6,000 jobs, but there was also a 66 percent chance that it would actually save *none* of the plants or jobs (Figure 1.3).

Executive Emotions Study

Gain Frame

74% **Plan A**
Save 1 out of 3 plants
and 2,000 jobs

26% **Plan B**
33% chance of saving
all of the plants/jobs
66% chance of saving
none of the plants/jobs

Loss Frame

Plan A
Lose 2 out of 3 plants
along w/4,000 jobs

Plan B
33% chance of losing
none of the plants/jobs
66% chance of losing
all of the plants/jobs

Figure 1.3 In the gain frame, only 26 percent chose the riskier option to achieve a gain.

Presented with these two plans, 74 percent chose the option presented in Plan A—saving one plant and 2,000 jobs. Only 26 percent chose Plan B—the riskier option that had a 33 percent chance of saving all the jobs and plants but a 66 percent chance that it might save none of the jobs or plants.

The second group of executives was presented with the exact same situation, but this time with a loss frame. Note that the math was exactly the same. Only the words were changed (Figure 1.4).

Executive Emotions Study

Gain Frame

 Plan A
Save 1 out of 3 plants
and 2,000 jobs

 Plan B
33% chance of saving
all of the plants/jobs
66% chance of saving
none of the plants/jobs

Loss Frame

 Plan A
Lose 2 out of 3 plants
along w/4,000 jobs

 Plan B
33% chance of losing
none of the plants/jobs
66% chance of losing
all of the plants/jobs

Figure 1.4 In the loss frame, 45 percent chose the riskier option to avoid a loss.

This second group saw Plan A framed as a loss statement, "Two out of three plants would be lost along with 4,000 jobs." And the same thing was changed about Plan B. The math for Plan B was the same for both groups, but in the second group the words were framed as a loss scenario: "A 66 percent chance of losing all three plants and 6,000 jobs. And a 33 percent chance of losing none of the plants and none of the jobs."

What's interesting is how the choices are different between the two groups. In this second group, when the status quo (Plan A) was framed as a loss, instead of 74 percent going with Plan A, now only 55 percent were willing to take that outcome. And look at the jump to Plan B! (See Figure 1.5.)

Executive Emotions Study

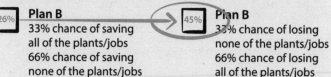

Gain Frame

74% **Plan A**
Save 1 out of 3 plants
and 2,000 jobs

Loss Frame

55% **Plan A**
Lose 2 out of 3 plants
along w/4,000 jobs

More than 70% increase in "persuadability"

26% **Plan B**
33% chance of saving
all of the plants/jobs
66% chance of saving
none of the plants/jobs

45% **Plan B**
33% chance of losing
none of the plants/jobs
66% chance of losing
all of the plants/jobs

Figure 1.5 "Persuadability" increased more than 70 percent in the loss frame.

Now 45 percent were willing to take the riskier bet of Plan B, even though the math across both Plan Bs (and Plan As) is exactly the same. In other words, you see a more than 70 percent increase in the "persuadability" of executives just by changing the story, not the math. Logically and mathematically, you would expect the same number of executives on both sides to choose Plan A and the same number to choose Plan B, but instead you see a huge change in the willingness of the executives to take a risk or seek a risk simply because of the way the status quo was framed.

Here's how to think about this: When you're the incumbent vendor, *you* are the status quo. And even if a competitor is telling an executive that it can do more for the executive's company than your company can, you're still in a very powerful position. What you need to do is frame your contribution in terms of the gains your customer gets by sticking with you. And you need to position your competitor's offering as possibly bringing some benefits but also a lot of risk. The psychological advantage with the executive is yours, if you can do that. From the other side, if you're trying to unseat a competitor, you need to first take the step of framing the act of sticking with the competitor as a loss for the executive, *before* framing the gains that you can bring.

You'll learn more about how to do that throughout this book. But suffice it to say that the next time someone tells you that executives make decisions purely rationally, "based on the math," don't let yourself be fooled. Even if it's the executives themselves who are telling you that.

DEFEATING STATUS QUO BIAS

Suppose you want to get a prospect to make a difficult change and choose you, or you want to get a new customer to adopt and use your new solution. Both are situations where you need to purposefully develop and deliver a Why Change story. And doing this successfully requires you to deliberately disrupt and

defeat the four causes of Status Quo Bias. To accomplish this—
to disrupt and defeat (see Figure 1.6)—you'll need to:

Defeat Status Quo Bias

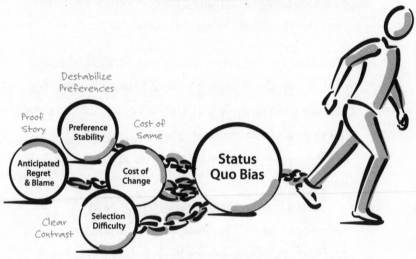

Figure 1.6. For an "acquisition" conversation,
disrupt and defeat the Status Quo Bias.

1. **Destabilize current preferences.** The only way
   to overcome Preference Stability is to deliberately
   destabilize your prospect's current preferences.
   Persuasion is only possible when prospects are
   uncertain about their current status quo. It's your job
   to introduce what we call "Unconsidered Needs" that
   help them see their status quo as unsafe.

   Unconsidered Needs can include problems,
   challenges, threats, or missed opportunities they
   weren't aware or didn't appreciate the significance of.

"Voice of the Customer" research, probing questions, and discovery calls are good at getting prospects to admit pains they know, but those are not significant enough to get them to change. Urgency is created only by telling them something they don't know about a situation they don't know they have.

2. **Show the cost of staying the same.** Since the burden of cost is on the change, you need to introduce the cost of staying the same. In fact, the cost of staying the same has to be equal to or greater than the Perceived Cost of Change for people to believe their status quo is no longer acceptable.

   Nobel Prize-winning research by Daniel Kahneman called "Prospect Theory" shows that people are two to three times more likely to make a change to avoid a loss than to get a potential gain. You must make sure that your story portrays the flaws and limitations in your prospect's current approach that will make it unscalable, untenable, or otherwise unacceptable cost-wise or loss-wise to keep doing the same thing.

3. **Introduce a clear contrasting alternative.** The decision-making part of the brain craves contrast. The perception of value—and the motivation for change—lies in the perceived contrast between how your prospect is struggling today and how much better they'll be doing with your solution in the future. No contrast, or not enough contrast, equals no perceived value for making the change.

The best way to communicate contrast is to show the clear risk associated with the prospect's current-state approach compared with the resolution to that risk provided by your recommended future-state solution.

4. **Demonstrate before and after proof.** A client testimonial or case study is the best way to overcome Anticipated Regret and Blame. For prospects, seeing someone else like them and their company successfully navigating the change management process and succeeding is critical to invoking the most powerful form of persuasion—self-persuasion. The key, however, is that your testimonial must contain both a before and after story.

   Too many case studies focus on just the successful outcomes. However, your prospects aren't ready for or looking for proof your solution works. They first need to believe they have a problem. Prospects living in Status Quo Bias must be treated like "deniers." They don't even know they have a problem worth solving. As a result, your customer example must clearly document and communicate the situation they were in, so your prospects can see themselves in the story.

The result of understanding and addressing the four causes of Status Quo Bias is a tested and proven Why Change story framework that marketers and salespeople at companies like yours have been using to develop and deliver customer acquisition messages with great success over the last few years (Figure 1.7).

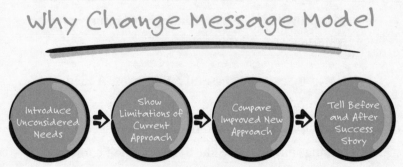

Why Change Message Model

Introduce Unconsidered Needs ➡ Show Limitations of Current Approach ➡ Compare Improved New Approach ➡ Tell Before and After Success Story

Figure 1.7 Use the Why Change message model to disrupt the status quo.

Our company has helped develop more than 1,000 Why Change messages for hundreds of companies, and we have trained more than 100,000 sellers on the skills necessary to tell a disruptive Why Change story in the most effective way.

In one of our most notable examples, a client company in the B2B payroll and benefits space identified 119 deals that had been marked "no decision" in its CRM system. The company retooled its story using the Why Change framework and relaunched it to its sales team. Within 90 days, the client had re-ignited 115 of those 119 deals and ended up closing millions of dollars of business that had once been considered lost.

Another company increased the "incident rate," or what other companies call a "close rate," by 40 percent by convincing 7 out of 10 new homeowners to purchase a fireplace when it had previously been 5 out of 10. The company was also able to increase the rate at which customers chose the premium fireplace option from 4 percent to 40 percent.

In both cases, the product didn't change. The sales team didn't change. The only thing that changed was the story, through the introduction of the Why Change message.

DON'T DISRUPT THE STATUS QUO
WHEN YOU ARE THE STATUS QUO

The successful deployment of all this Why Change messaging raised a persistent follow-on question from our customers: "This is all very well and good. But should we use this approach when we're trying to renew business with existing customers?"

For years, whenever our clients challenged us with this question, we weren't sure how to answer. You can make a good, logical case that using the same provocative, insight-laden message with existing customers that you used with prospects ought to produce the same results. After all, a sales motion is a sales motion, whether it's to a new prospect or to an existing customer, isn't it? Also, you want your existing customers to continue to think of your company as a thought leader, so doesn't that mean you should bring them that provocative thought leadership at the time of renewal? And after all, your customers' world is always changing, so it seems logical to believe that a change message would always be the right one.

This was one set of thoughts going through our heads. But there was another countervailing narrative going through our heads at the same time. As disciples of the Decision Sciences, we knew that it's all too easy to believe a narrative without doing real-world research to confirm whether or not your belief is correct. And we are committed to only giving recommendations based on things we've confirmed through rigorous testing, as opposed to simply offering our best guess. So the question we needed to answer was, is it just as effective to use the same message you used to sell to a new prospect when selling to an existing customer?

Our research proved otherwise. And of course made us glad that we don't make it a practice to offer opinions in the absence of data.

As our scientist partners put it, after multiple tests to make sure the findings were right, "It's called Status Quo Bias for a reason." It's real. It's powerful. So when you are the status quo, lean into it, reinforce it, and deliberately leverage it to your advantage (Figure 1.8).

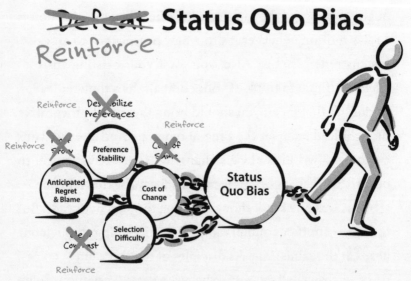

Figure 1.8 For an "expansion" conversation, reinforce Status Quo Bias.

Here's a quick overview of how you need to reinforce the four causes of Status Quo Bias to deliver a compelling retention message:

1. **Preference Stability.** Make a point of reminding customers of the long, hard process they went through to make their original buying decision. This will reinforce their natural tendency to keep their previous decisions and preferences stable.

2. **Perceived Cost of Change.** Walk customers through the start-up costs that have now been returned through improved performance and are now "sunk" and functionally part of the ongoing operating budget. People tend to believe change costs more than staying the same—confirm that.

3. **Selection Difficulty.** Willingly admit that most other solutions on the market provide a similar set of capabilities, that the offerings haven't changed significantly since their original decision, and that you've kept both your customers and your solutions updated throughout your journey together. People are less likely to consider change if they don't discern contrast between the alternatives.

4. **Anticipated Regret and Blame.** Remind customers of the time and resources it's taken to ramp up the solution they purchased, onboard all their people, manage the changes, and get the implementation

running smoothly. Making another change exposes them to all these potential failure points again, which they could get blamed for.

You'll find more specific story-building and storytelling techniques in the following chapters as you learn the frameworks for the four must-win commercial moments in customer expansion.

2

Expansion Messaging

Mission Critical, but Missing in Action

arketing, sales, and customer success have a pretty straightforward mission: Identify the best customers in your "sweet spot"—the ones who can deliver the most value over the long haul—and then sell and service the heck out of them. How this actually gets executed might vary from company to company, but the core objective always remains the same.

Here's the conundrum: It costs a lot of money to attract and land these coveted customers. It costs even more to onboard them. And if you offer deep discounts to win the business and then overservice them to ensure a great initial experience, as many organizations do, your start-up costs will be even higher.

That means that for many organizations, especially those that sell subscription-type contracts, the real profitability doesn't kick in until you score that first renewal.

Interestingly, though, while it's useful to think about this in terms of your own cost outlays and profitability—and this framing certainly bolsters *your* need for a powerful expansion message—there are cost and profitability considerations for the customers as well. In fact, your incumbency can benefit them just as much as it benefits you.

THE POWER OF INCUMBENCY

Every customer-vendor relationship boils down to value over time. After the deal is signed, your customer should start receiving some initial value in terms of business impact and results (Figure 2.1). Granted, progress might be minimal at first, but the customer should be realizing some benefit. That's progress the client should be loath to give up by making a change at the wrong time.

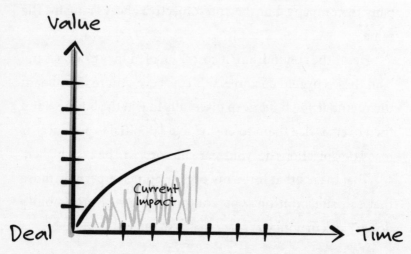

Figure 2.1 Customers receive initial value after the deal is signed.

But it's not all upside. Your customers have invested time, money, and political capital in getting your solution up and running. In their minds, these are sunk costs—investments they've made that they'll never have to make again . . . *provided* they stick with you.

This is your "Incumbent Advantage" (Figure 2.2).

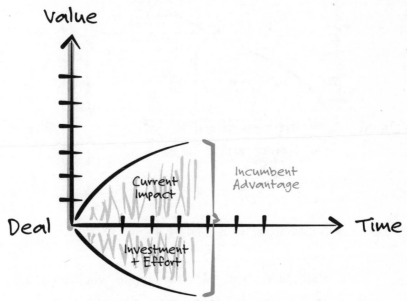

Figure 2.2 Incumbent Advantage kicks in when "sunk cost" mentality takes hold.

When a competitor shows up promising additional value, it's really only *potential* value. The competitor's solution is still unproven, the cost and impact are both unknown, and change comes at the risk of the initial progress as well as any future value from your solution. That's a lot of uncertainty compared with your documented value and the customer's sunk cost. In other words, you need to position your incumbency as the sure bet and your competitor's offering as the risk (Figure 2.3).

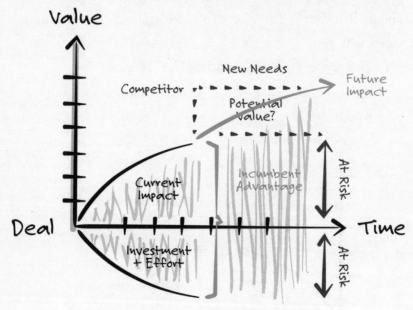

Figure 2.3 Your incumbency is the "sure bet," while the competitive offering is unproven and a risk.

Incidentally, Incumbent Advantage applies whether you're trying to get your customers to renew or repurchase an existing solution or if you want them to expand their business with you. In either case, just like in politics, it can be very hard to displace an incumbent because of all the advantages the incumbent has in terms of name recognition, publicity, experience, track record, and, of course, good old Status Quo Bias.

Unfortunately, too many companies squander their Incumbent Advantage and, in doing so, let their competition into the conversation. In fact, not only do they fail to exploit their Incumbent Advantage; they unintentionally undermine it in three key areas.

THEY UNDERINVEST IN RETENTION

According to a Corporate Visions survey of more than 400 B2B organizations, 80 percent of companies spend more than 70 percent of their sales and marketing budget on demand generation messaging, content marketing, and sales enablement and management for new customer acquisition. Retention and expansion programming fight it out for the other 30 percent. What's more, nearly half of the companies surveyed invest less than 10 percent of their marketing and sales budgets in retention, renewal, and upselling/cross-selling (Figure 2.4).

How much of your budget is attributed to customer retention and upsell/cross-sell?

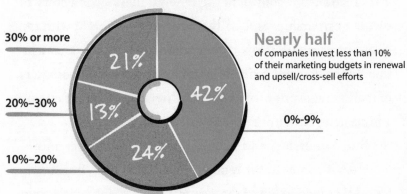

30% or more — 21%

20%–30% — 13%

10%–20% — 24%

42%

Nearly half
of companies invest less than 10% of their marketing budgets in renewal and upsell/cross-sell efforts

0%-9%

Corporate Visions Survey: *From Lead to Advocacy: What's in Your Customer Lifecycle Message?*, January 2017

Figure 2.4 Companies underinvest in retention, renewal, and upsell/add-on sales.

Turning prime prospects into new opportunities is exciting, especially when the prospects fit the profile of your most loyal long-term buyers. No wonder companies pour the lion's share of money and effort into the first part of the buyer's journey—the sexy, swashbuckling customer acquisition message—even though they reap as much as 80 percent of their revenue from existing customers. Conquest is just more fun.

But consider the impact that has on profitability—and, yes, this calls for more math. Given that a variety of studies have shown that a small increase in retention can boost profitability significantly, wouldn't it make sense to funnel *more* of your sales and marketing budget in that direction? Conversely, how much profit are you giving up by underfunding your retention message?

THERE'S NO CLEAR OWNERSHIP OF THE RENEWAL MESSAGE

The creation and control of the renewal message is a story of divided ownership, especially when you compare it with the clear-cut world of demand generation and customer acquisition. In the demand generation universe, nearly three-quarters of marketing teams own or share ownership of the messaging and content. No surprise there.

But ownership and accountability become far murkier when it comes to the renewal message. In fact, our survey found that ownership of the renewal story varies wildly from company to company. In half of the companies we surveyed, marketing isn't involved at all, with ownership falling either to sales/business development/sales enablement (28 percent) or to related account management teams (21 percent). In 19 percent of companies, on the other hand, marketing owns this messaging exclusively (Figure 2.5).

Who owns message and content development?

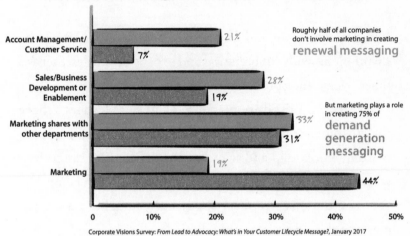

Corporate Visions Survey: *From Lead to Advocacy: What's in Your Customer Lifecycle Message?*, January 2017

Figure 2.5 With no clear ownership of the renewal message, lack of clarity and consistency undercut Incumbent Advantage.

When there's no clear ownership of a message, there's less accountability and fewer guardrails around how that story gets created. That means inconsistent quality and an overall decrease in message effectiveness. And with fragmented owner-ship comes fragmented delivery. With so many different teams interacting with a customer (sales, customer success, customer service, implementation, to name a few), the less discipline that's applied to message creation, the less discipline is applied to what message is ultimately communicated.

At a time when renewal business is so critical to growth and long-term value, lack of clarity around the message increases confusion and undercuts your entire organization's ability to reinforce and build on your Incumbent Advantage.

THEY DON'T DISTINGUISH BETWEEN ACQUISITION AND EXPANSION MESSAGING

If underinvestment and fragmented ownership are the tactical problems with your renewal and expansion stories, there's a third, overarching problem: the message itself.

Nearly two-thirds of marketing and sales leaders believe the customer conversation is the leading driver of competitive differentiation,* and so messaging deficiencies can be fatal when you're trying to renew or expand a customer relationship. Yet organizations give surprisingly little thought to what that message should be. Not only do the majority of respondents (58 percent according to the Corporate Visions survey) believe there should be no need to differentiate messaging between acquisition and expansion; they also believe that a provocative, disruptive message is appropriate for a renewal scenario (Figure 2.6).

At this point, you already know from your understanding of Status Quo Bias that if 58 percent want a provocative message for retention, that's 58 percent too much! This means that not only are your teams out there delivering the wrong message to existing customers; they're delivering one that actively undermines your commercial success and obliterates your Incumbent Advantage.

---

* Sales Messaging Survey, Corporate Visions, 2015.

Do you think your messaging and content for demand generation/ customer acquisition strategies should differ from your messaging for retention/renewal business?

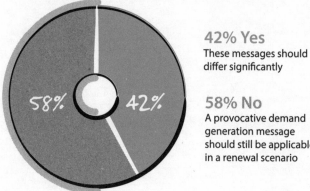

42% Yes
These messages should differ significantly

58% No
A provocative demand generation message should still be applicable in a renewal scenario

Corporate Visions Survey: *From Lead to Advocacy: What's in Your Customer Lifecycle Message?*, January 2017

Figure 2.6. The majority of companies believe a provocative message is appropriate for a renewal conversation—to their detriment.

Clearly, there's a better approach—one that sales, marketing, and customer success can unify around. The rest of this book is dedicated to those of you who want to find that better way.

3

Why Stay and the Psychology Behind Renewals

When you're messaging to new prospects, you're trying to disrupt their status quo. That means that before you can make the case for choosing you, you must first make the case for change. But as you saw in the previous chapters, that edgy, disruptive message you used to bring them in the door undermines your primary advantage when it comes to existing customers—your incumbency.

So what is the best way to capitalize on your Incumbent Advantage and deliver a message that reinforces, rather than disrupts, the status quo?

That's what our Why Stay Renewal Study aimed to find out.

THE WHY STAY RENEWAL STUDY

Together with Dr. Zakary Tormala, we tested three types of messages to determine which would be most effective in a hypothetical renewal scenario.

At the outset of the study, participants were instructed to imagine that they ran a small business and that two years ago they had signed up with a 401k provider to help promote their company's retirement plan to employees. Their objective was to boost employee satisfaction and retention by getting more people to sign up.

Participants were also told that two years ago only 20 percent of their employees subscribed to the 401k plan, against a goal of 80 percent. Now, two years later, participation had risen to 50 percent—higher than the previous 20 percent but still short of the 80 percent target. Meanwhile, employee retention rates had improved, but it was difficult to know how much of that was attributable to promoting the 401k plan.

The participants were divided across each of the three approaches, or study conditions. They only got to view and listen to one type of renewal pitch. The opening paragraph of each pitch was identical across the three conditions, but then each of the pitches varied in crucial ways:

- **Pitch #1: Status Quo Reinforcement.** Participants in this group received an encouraging description of how the plan was working to date and heard how the company was progressing toward its goals. They also read a message intended to reinforce the status quo, emphasizing how much effort went into selecting the current provider and highlighting the risks and costs associated with switching to a new one.

- **Pitch #2: Provocative Why Change Pitch.** This message documented the results to date but then switched gears, introducing a new idea that challenged the current approach. This message noted that it can be harder to make the jump from 50 percent to 80 percent participation than it is to go from 20 percent to 50 percent, and that doing so may require different tactics, such as switching the 401k plan from an "opt-in" approach to an "opt-out" one. The provider would help make this change.

- **Pitch 3: Provocative Pitch with Upsell.** This message was the same as the provocative pitch above, except it also offered a selection of new online tools to help engage employees in reaching their goals. The new tools would add 5 percent to the overall program costs, with an anticipated payback in fewer than 12 months.

After hearing their respective message, participants answered a series of questions designed to assess their reactions to the message and its persuasive impact. The questions focused on participants' intention to renew, attitudes toward the provider, likeliness to switch, and credibility.

REINFORCING STATUS QUO BIAS: WHAT THE RESEARCH REVEALED

Across the measures assessed in the experiment, the status quo reinforcement message outperformed both the provocative and the provocative with upsell message by significant margins.

The message that documented success and reinforced the Status Quo Bias delivered the following results:

- **13 percent boost in intention to renew** relative to the two provocative messages. To measure this, participants were asked how likely they would be to renew with their current provider and how likely it was that they'd stick with that provider (Figure 3.1).

- **9 percent boost in positive attitudes** compared with the other two pitches. Participants had significantly more favorable impressions of the provider than in either of the message conditions that challenged the current approach with a new idea.

- **7 percent lift in credibility perceptions** relative to the provocative conditions. Participants answered three questions assessing how credible, trustworthy, and confidence-inspiring the provider seemed to be.

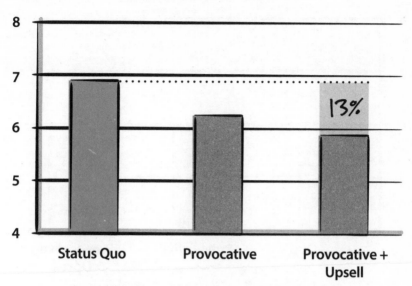

Figure 3.1 The status quo reinforcement message outperformed the provocative messages by 13 percent when it came to "intention to renew."

Most importantly, when participants answered three questions designed to measure switching intentions—that is, how likely they would be to shop around for alternatives or even switch to a new provider—the results were significant (Figure 3.2). *Participants in the provocative conditions were 10 percent more likely to switch or shop around than participants in the condition that documented success and reinforced the status quo.*

Turns out, when you're the status quo, the biggest risk of using a disruptive message is that it will work!

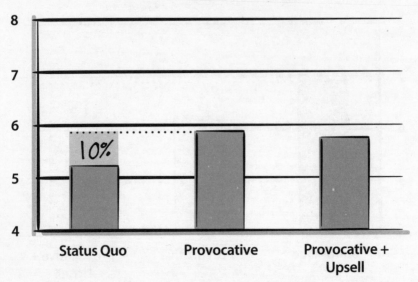

Figure 3.2 Participants who received the provocative message were 10 percent more likely to switch than those who received the status quo reinforcement message.

WHAT'S IN A WINNING WHY STAY MESSAGE?

The message framework that had the most powerful impact on the renewal decision took participants through a systematic reinforcement of their natural Status Quo Bias—reaffirming each of the four antecedents you read about in Chapter 1 (see Figure 3.3).

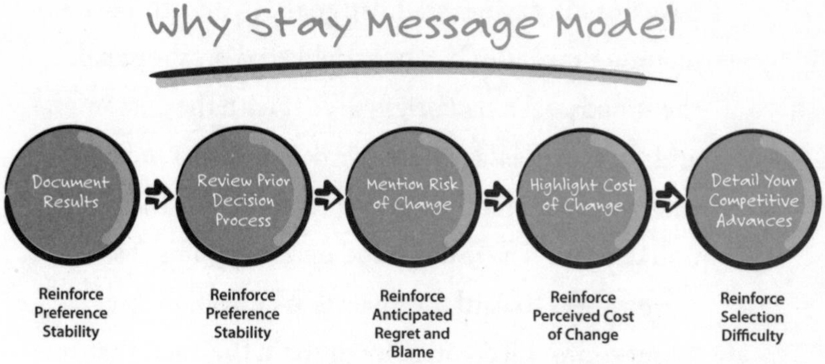

Why Stay Message Model

Document Results	Review Prior Decision Process	Mention Risk of Change	Highlight Cost of Change	Detail Your Competitive Advances
Reinforce Preference Stability	Reinforce Preference Stability	Reinforce Anticipated Regret and Blame	Reinforce Perceived Cost of Change	Reinforce Selection Difficulty

Figure 3.3 Use the Why Stay message model to reinforce Status Quo Bias and win the renewal.

Here's the narrative, along with our analysis of why each element worked as a component of a renewal message:

1. **Document results (reinforce Preference Stability).**
   You've made great progress on your goals over these last two years. You've seen 401k participation grow from 20 percent to 50 percent. Your employee satisfaction scores are up, and your employee retention rates have started to improve, which was the ultimate goal of making these changes.

   Showing the results you've helped your customer achieve is a great way to put everyone in a good mood to kick off a renewal meeting. But there's a practical reason for documenting results as well: credibility. The participants in our study reported greater trust in the provider when the provider's message first documented results. Customers need to hear this assessment before they'll be receptive to the rest of your message.

   Hearing about progress to their goals also reinforces Preference Stability, even though they likely have not fully achieved those goals. In our study, the incumbent vendor had only delivered on about half the stated goal it had originally set with the customer, and yet that message framework still won. Our hope is, you'll do better than 50 percent, but it's still highly unlikely you'll have delivered on everything. It's the progress toward the goals that customers care about—provided you're focused on the goals that are important to them. While it might be tempting, in the heat of preparation for a QBR or a renewal meeting, to highlight the goals that show the most progress, in reality you should choose the ones your customers consider the most important.

2. **Review the prior decision process (reinforce Preference Stability).** *When you signed up two years ago, you really did your homework and looked at a lot of options before getting your entire team to come to a consensus and choose our company.*

By reminding the customers of the process they went through to choose you, you reinforce Preference Stability in two ways. First, you reaffirm that they did their due diligence during the selection process. Did they issue an RFP? Did they invite executive sponsors to buying committee meetings? Did they do a pilot or a proof of concept? If so, they can rest assured they did a thorough evaluation. And second, by taking them back through every step of their decision, you're gently reminding them of how agonizing that process was. Why in the world would they want to repeat it—

especially if they're going to end up with something that's "just like" what they're already doing with you?

3. **Mention the risk of change (reinforce Anticipated Regret and Blame).** *As you look at making a renewal decision, it's important to realize that you are at a critical point in this journey and that it's important to maintain momentum to achieve your ultimate participation and retention goals. Any change in the program at this point could create an unnecessary risk of losing the positive gains you've made.*

   This step is meant to trigger Anticipated Regret and Blame, and it works in lockstep with the Incumbent Advantage concept we described in Chapter 2, as well as with your customers' natural loss aversion. Not only will switching to an unproven solution increase the risk that something could go terribly wrong; it could also erase the progress they've already made to the goals you just documented.

4. **Highlight the cost of change (reinforce Perceived Cost of Change).** *Bringing in another vendor would require you to invest both time in getting the vendor up to speed and money on implementation costs and other changes that you won't have to spend if you continue working with us.*

   Even if none of the risks above ever materialize, or your customers aren't worried about them, change still carries a cost. Your competitor might be trying to undercut you on price, but your customers' Status Quo Bias is still telling them that doing nothing is the less expensive option—and who are you to argue with that? Nudge them along. Educate them about all the ancillary costs that are not in the competitor's quote. Do they need to replace equipment, integrate systems, redesign business processes, train their staff? Will they need to notify customers and vendors? Will they have to run both systems concurrently during the switchover? All this takes time and resources, which can quickly eat away any difference in the quoted price. Your competitor certainly won't mention any of this, so your customers won't have the full picture unless you bring it up.

5. **Detail competitive advances (reinforce Selection Difficulty).** *We've continued to update your program over the last two years to ensure you're keeping pace with anything else available in the market today. You'll get two new features to help improve your goals of employee participation and satisfaction: a monthly report showing tax dollars 401k participants saved vs. those not in the plan, and an app with retirement planning calculators and budgeting tools to help your employees make more informed decisions.*

Take a look at the wording above. As you saw in Chapter 1, Selection Difficulty says that if customers perceive all options as equal, they'll stick with the status quo—in this case, you. You also saw earlier in this chapter that using a disruptive message can compel your customers to look at other options. So how do you show your customers you're continuing to innovate?

The answer is, you introduce new capabilities in the context of the original problems the customers were trying to solve. You don't want to put it in the context of some new, previously Unconsidered Need. You want the new capabilities to appear as an extension and continuation of the customers moving toward their original goals. This is a tough rule to follow if you're a marketer or seller expected to tout how "revolutionary" or "cutting edge" your new capabilities are. It's not that it's not okay to be proud of your new stuff. You can even say it's better than the competitor's. Just don't describe it as a game-changing disruption no one's ever thought of before. That's practically begging your customers to go out and try to prove you wrong.

What do you do if you have something that actually is a game changer, though? Then it's a question of timing. If you have a committed contract with a customer, with plenty of time left, then it's safe to introduce that new capability. But if you're close to a renewal date, you might have missed your window. The best thing you can do at that point is to place the new feature in the context of the original problems the customer was trying to solve, secure the renewal, and then introduce the Unconsidered Needs that the new feature will address when you're safely in the new contract term.

That might be counterintuitive. But by now you know the risk of being too disruptive with an existing customer.

4

Cracking the Code
on the Price Increase
Conversation

I t's hard enough to get your customer to keep buying the same solution from you. Luckily, you now have a handy, scientifically tested message framework to support your renewal conversations.

But if you're like the folks in any other organization, you're not just looking to renew that business. Sooner or later, you're going to have to ask people to pay more. This is borne out by our own research: In a survey of more than 300 B2B organizations, we found that nearly two-thirds (63 percent) consider price increases "very important" or even "mission critical" for maintaining client profitability and driving overall growth.

That means that in addition to navigating that tricky renewal conversation, you're also going to have to manage a far more delicate, complex, and politically fraught discussion: the price increase.

It's a high-stakes conversation that has huge ramifications for your bottom line. In fact, in 2014 Bain & Company noted that pricing has a more profound business impact than gaining market share or reducing costs.* So companies treat pricing with the appropriate reverence, investing in pricing departments staffed with market researchers, analysts, and data scientists busily developing models and algorithms to try to optimize pricing. But analyses and algorithms can only give you the rationale. If you don't communicate that price change effectively, it will undoubtedly fail in the market.

That's the lesson from the second part of our survey, which revealed, among other challenges, that companies lack the confidence, messaging structure, and communication strategy needed to effectively communicate price increases to their customers.

A QUESTION OF CONFIDENCE

Nearly 69 percent of respondents describe customers' reception to news of a price increase as "50-50 or worse"—in other words, sometimes it goes over well, other times not so well (Figure 4.1).

It also means that only about a third of companies believe their price increase conversations go the way they want, by either getting an acceptable increase (26 percent) or getting everything they wanted (5 percent). That's not exactly a glow-

---

* Stephen Mewborn, Justin Murphy, and Glen Williams, *Clearing the Roadblocks to Better B2B Pricing*, Bain & Company, 2014.

ing endorsement of how the average company is handling this dialogue at an acute commercial moment, and it shows there's plenty of room for improvement.

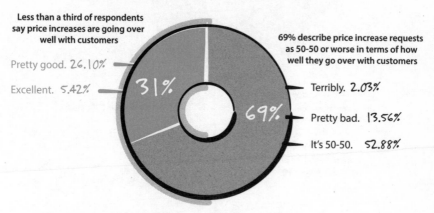

When you communicate price increases to your customers, how well does it go over?

Less than a third of respondents say price increases are going over well with customers

Pretty good. 26.10%

Excellent. 5.42%

31%

69% describe price increase requests as 50-50 or worse in terms of how well they go over with customers

69%

Terribly. 2.03%

Pretty bad. 13.56%

It's 50-50. 52.88%

Figure 4.1 Price increase communications don't go over well with customers—most report "50-50 or worse."

If these important discussions are not going as planned, it's no wonder survey respondents admitted feeling shaky when asked about their confidence level in the way they're communicating price increases: Just 37 percent are "confident" in their approach, and only 8 percent feel "very confident." This leaves the majority—55 percent—feeling unsure about their price increase messaging (Figure 4.2).

So what's going wrong?

How confident are you that the way you structure and deliver
your price increase message is the most effective for communicating price
increases and creating positive outcomes?

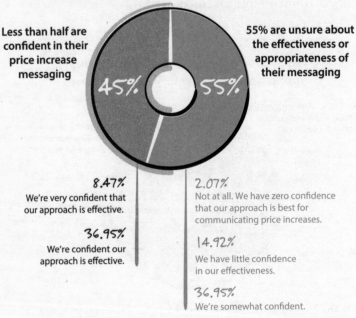

**Less than half are
confident in their
price increase
messaging**

45%

55%

**55% are unsure about
the effectiveness or
appropriateness of
their messaging**

8.47%
We're very confident that
our approach is effective.

36.95%
We're confident our
approach is effective.

2.07%
Not at all. We have zero confidence
that our approach is best for
communicating price increases.

14.92%
We have little confidence
in our effectiveness.

36.95%
We're somewhat confident.

Figure 4.2 Less than half are confident their price increase
messages are effective or appropriate.

A STRUCTURAL FLAW

One factor causing many companies to underperform in their
price increase conversations could be the lack of messaging
structure guiding them. In our survey, fewer than one-third of
respondents (32 percent) said they believe their approach to
communicating price increases is "highly structured"—meaning they craft a deliberate communication plan using persuasive
messaging techniques and support those who own the responsibility with the skills necessary to support those conversations.

Among the other two-thirds of companies struggling with messaging structure, the survey found that:

- 23 percent admit it's ad hoc, meaning they have no formal approach in place for this conversation and leave it to the responsible parties to develop and deliver the increase message to customers.

- 44 percent say their approach is "somewhat" structured, meaning someone creates a formal communication so the story is consistent but then either leaves the actual delivery up to the responsible parties or sends the customer an e-mail notification with limited direction to the teams responsible for following up.

What's clear is there's a definite appetite among B2B practitioners for more rigor around the price increase message. In fact, nearly 80 percent of companies surveyed say they want to make their price increase requests more formal and strategic. Interestingly, these respondents split into three camps:

1. Those who want more structure but have not made it a priority (40 percent)

2. Those who strongly desire a formalized structure, a message framework, and skills training to improve these communications (21 percent)

3. Those who fall somewhere between these two in terms of their desire for a more formal strategic approach (18 percent)

In other words, there are plenty of people looking for a better way. But there's no clear consensus around what that better way might be.

COMMUNICATION IS ACCIDENTAL, NOT PURPOSEFUL

In Chapter 3, you saw that ownership of the renewal message varies wildly from company to company. When it comes to price increases, it appears, at least at first glance, that there's more clarity: We found that sales is responsible for communicating price increases at 60 percent of the companies we surveyed (Figure 4.3). But if 80 percent of companies believe they need a more formal and strategic approach for messaging price increases, one has to wonder how purposeful that responsibility is. Could the responsibility have simply defaulted to sales because no one else is paying attention to it?

With more organizations building customer success teams, often with direct renewal and price increase targets, ownership becomes even murkier. While the people in customer success might be tasked with the day-to-day customer communications, they often hand off the "tough conversations," e.g., price increases, to their sales counterparts—preferring instead to focus on activities directly related to customer satisfaction.

But without clear-cut ownership of this conversation, the odds of a poorly communicated, less-than-optimal price increase message increase dramatically.

Which department in your company has the PRIMARY responsibility for communicating price increases to customers?

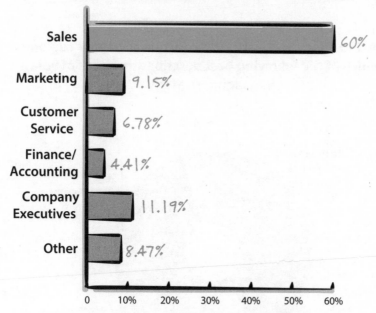

Figure 4.3 The job of communicating the price increase is usually left to sales—but is that by accident or by design?

WHAT APPROACHES ARE COMPANIES TAKING?

In our survey, we defined the six different messaging approaches our own clients use most frequently in their price increase conversations. We then asked respondents to identify which best describes their own approach.

Ultimately, as indicated in Figure 4.4, no single approach dominates. While it's clear that companies are trying different tactics, there appears to be a lingering question around what works best. (*Spoiler Alert:* The two least-used approaches below turned out to be the *most effective* approaches in our simulation—more on that in Chapter 5.)

As you introduce and justify price increases to your customers, which of the following best describes the focus of your messaging strategy?

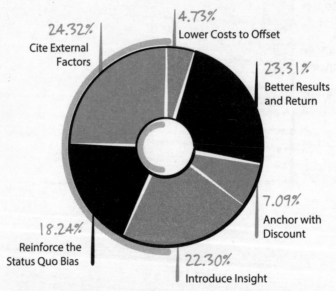

Figure 4.4 Since no single approach dominates, it's likely a substantial proportion are getting the conversation wrong.

Here are the six approaches we asked about in our survey and later tested in our research simulation:

1. **Offset price increase by lowering other costs.** Introduce new features and benefits to demonstrate how these improvements will lower other costs, thus offsetting some of the price increase.

2. **Justify price increase through better results and higher returns.** Introduce new features and benefits and explain how these will drive better business results, thus justifying the price increase.

3. **Anchor higher price with timed discount.** Introduce new features and benefits to justify the price increase, but offer a time-sensitive discount on the higher price.

4. **Introduce insight (using provocative Why Change message model).** Introduce Unconsidered Needs and show how new capabilities will solve them and deliver better performance, thus justifying the price increase.

5. **Secure price increase by reinforcing Status Quo Bias (using Why Stay message model).** Document results and revisit the selection process; then present the price increase as one that's competitive with the industry.

6. **Cite external costs as a reason for price increase.** Reference external factors (e.g., economy, operational costs, higher supplier prices, increased raw materials costs, etc.) as the reason for the price increase.

All of the above approaches certainly have some grounding in reality—as you see from the distribution of responses. But the wide variance reported indicates that no one knows for sure which approach is most effective, which means a substantial proportion of organizations are most likely getting the conver-

sation wrong. It remains an under-studied, untested component of the customer conversation—and one in dire need of a
scientifically tested message framework.

In other words, an area ripe for exploration.

5

Why Pay More

A Framework for Improving Your Price Increase Conversations

Since only 8 percent of companies are "very confident" in their price increase conversations and nearly four out of five companies want a more structured, rigorous approach, it's past time to ask whether there's an appetite for improvement. In partnership with Dr. Nick Lee of Warwick Business School, we set out to analyze the effectiveness of the six approaches detailed in Chapter 4, with an eye toward discovering which delivered the most favorable outcomes—that is, which was best for communicating a price increase while minimizing the risk of dissatisfaction and defection. This distinction is important, because we didn't approach this study looking for a message that would lead a customer to exclaim, "Yes! Now that I understand it, I'm really glad you're raising my price!"

The six approaches were inserted into the following scenario:

Participants were told to imagine they were small-business owners nearing the end of a two-year contract with a vendor they'd hired to promote their company's health and wellness program to employees, a move designed to improve employee satisfaction and retention rates. It was time to either renew with the existing vendor—*at a 4 percent price increase*—or consider switching to a new vendor.

All the test conditions in this experiment included the same 4 percent price increase. In addition, they all opened the same way by documenting the same business results achieved during the first term of the contract (an element essential to a favorable renewal). From there, the test conditions varied based on the approach:

1. **Unconsidered Needs (Why Change message model).** This scenario assumed a price increase would be more palatable if the customers saw it as part of a significant change and update to their solution. The message introduced new research revealing an alternative approach to plan participation that would require additional services that cost 4 percent more. The message also assured the customers they would recover that price increase within a year, based on improved program performance. So they'd pay more, but they'd get necessary capabilities and a calculated payback on the additional costs.

2. **Improved capabilities with a pricing anchor.** This test condition described additional new capabilities and improvements that would be included with the renewal. It described how the new capabilities

would increase performance and progress toward the customer's top goals. It also explained that these new capabilities would ordinarily add 8 percent to the annual program cost; however, existing customers would have that increase halved to 4 percent for being loyal customers. The net price increase was the same 4 percent as the rest of the test conditions offered, but it was presented with a high "anchoring" increase and a loyal customer discount.

3. **Improved capabilities without a pricing anchor.** This test condition mirrored the one above, except without "anchoring" the higher price point. It simply presented the new capabilities and performance as a justification for a straight-up 4 percent price increase.

4. **Improved capabilities with a time-sensitive discount.** This test condition introduced the improved capabilities and described how they would improve performance, as detailed above, and acknowledged that the new capabilities would add 8 percent to the annual cost. But in this case, it offered a time-sensitive discount—a 50 percent reduction in the increase (for a net 4 percent increase) provided the customer renewed by the end of the month. Since many companies rely on this approach to spur customers to renew quickly, we were curious to see how well it would perform in a controlled test against other approaches.

5. **External cost factors.** This message cited external costs as the reason for the increase—specifically, regulations and mandated changes that added cost to the vendor supplier that necessitated an 8 percent cost increase. In a goodwill gesture, this approach used an anchor, explaining the vendor would absorb half the extra cost burden but must pass along the remaining 4 percent to the customer. This is a very real and common justification for a price increase, so we were interested in seeing how the "excuse" approach would fare against others.

6. **Status Quo Bias reinforcement (Why Stay message model).** This scenario framed the price increase in the winning Why Stay message approach. It assumed that reinforcing the Status Quo Bias, and reminding customers of the potential risks and costs associated with bringing in a new vendor, could also work in a price increase setting. In this message, we took a very conservative approach and communicated a straight 4 percent price increase with no anchoring.

Understanding the Anchoring Effect

The "anchoring effect" is a cognitive bias that causes you to rely heavily on the first piece of information you receive. When people are faced with a decision that involves some type of uncertainty, they'll anchor on a reference point and ascribe value based on that.

In his book *Pre-Suasion*, Dr. Robert Cialdini shares a story about a consultant meeting with a client to demonstrate how you can influence people in advance. The client voices concern about the potential cost of the engagement, and the consultant replies, "Well, it's not going to be a million dollars." (Historically, he was lucky to get an engagement at $250,000–$300,000.) The client, anchored on the $1 million figure, agreed to do the engagement for $700,000. The client was happy because it did not cost him $1 million, and the consultant was happy because it was more than twice the cost of his typical deal.*

What does this mean for your price increase message?

Before you tell your customers about your price increase, they're already anchored on a number. Where does that anchor come from? If you're messaging it right—*you*. By setting the reference point for the customers, you're better able to influence their perception of your price increase and thus how well they respond to it.

THE RESULTS

Every test condition asked for the same 4 percent increase. And each condition opened by documenting the same business results achieved during the first contract term.

---

* Robert B. Cialdini, *Pre-Suasion: A Revolutionary Way to Influence and Persuade*, 2016.

But this study showed clear winners and losers.

The biggest loser was the "Unconsidered Needs" approach modeled against the Why Change message. It finished dead last in every category:

- Participants who heard the price increase in the Why Change context had an *18.8 percent less favorable attitude* toward the vendor compared with the winning approach (Figure 5.1).

- They were also *15.5 percent less likely to renew* with their current vendor compared with the winning message (Figure 5.2).

- And they were *16.3 percent more likely to switch to a competitor* offering discounted pricing (Figure 5.3).

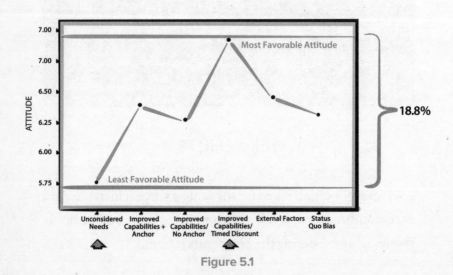

Figure 5.1

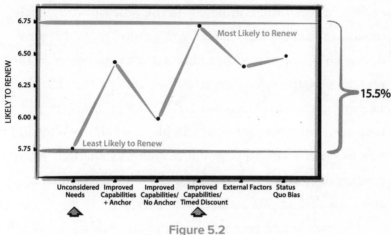

Figure 5.2

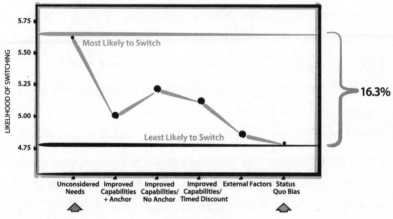

Figure 5.3

Figures 5.1–5.3 Why Change messaging loses big in a renewal scenario—finishing dead last in favorable attitude toward vendor and likelihood to renew and finishing first in switching likelihood.

Why would this last condition perform so poorly? One would assume that if you're offering new capabilities the customers don't currently have, they'd see all sorts of new value ... right?

If you recall the findings from the renewal study documented in the previous chapter, you will also recall that introducing an Unconsidered Need had a detrimental effect on the renewal message. According to our research partner, Dr. Nick Lee, introducing the Unconsidered Need would likely provoke customers to "think more carefully about what they want and how to get it." By disrupting your customer's status quo, you're creating discomfort and prompting them to reassess their situation—including your status as their provider.

Meanwhile, the winning price increase message appears to embody two things: First, it reinforces the status quo while introducing competitive advances that align with the customer's business goals. Second, it anchors high with the new price before giving the justified discount to secure the renewal.

The "external factors" condition is notable, because in the survey cited in the previous chapter this was the most commonly used strategy. While this strategy did reasonably well, it was outperformed in every category. When we ask our clients why they prefer this strategy, they say it shows the price increase is beyond their control and thus "not their fault." This is an understandable instinct, and it might feel better to tell your customers you wish you didn't have to do this. But put yourself in your customer's position. They're still getting a price increase. It might not be your fault, but it's still their problem.

So what was the winning condition? Per the results above (Figures 5.1–5.3), the Why Stay message, coupled with the timed discount, performed the best.

THE WINNING WHY PAY MORE CONDITION

The research confirms that, much like a compelling customer retention message, an effective price increase message will document proven business results, reinforce Status Quo Bias, detail competitive advances that improve performance against original business needs and goals, and anchor a price increase but then offer a loyalty discount (Figure 5.4).

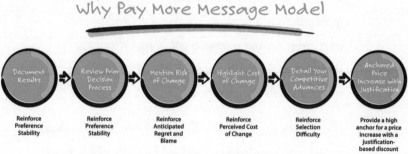

Why Pay More Message Model

Document Results	Review Prior Decision Process	Mention Risk of Change	Highlight Cost of Change	Detail Your Competitive Advances	Anchored Price Increase with Justification
Reinforce Preference Stability	Reinforce Preference Stability	Reinforce Anticipated Regret and Blame	Reinforce Perceived Cost of Change	Reinforce Selection Difficulty	Provide a high anchor for a price increase with a justification-based discount

Figure 5.4 Use the Why Pay More message model to keep your customers buying, and paying more for, their existing solution.

Here's the actual text of the winning approach:

1. **Document results.** *You have made great progress on your goals over these last two years. You've seen health and wellness program participation grow from 20 percent to 50 percent. Your employee satisfaction scores are up, and you've said some employees have even taken the time to thank you for the changes you've made. In addition, your employee retention rates have started to improve, which you said was the ultimate goal of making these changes.*

2. **Review the prior decision process.** *When you signed up two years ago, you really did your homework and looked at a lot of options before getting your entire team to come to a consensus and choose our company. It was a long process that involved a lot of people, but you ultimately arrived at a big decision to bring this program on board.*

3. **Mention the risk of change.** *As you look at making a renewal decision, it's important to realize that you are at a critical point in this journey and that it's important to maintain momentum to achieve your ultimate participation and retention goals. Any change to the program at this point could create an unnecessary risk of losing the positive gains you've made.*

4. **Highlight the cost of change.** *Not to mention that bringing in another vendor would require you to invest both time in getting the vendor up to speed and money on implementation costs and other changes that you won't have to spend if you continue working with us.*

5. **Detail competitive advances.** *Over the last two years we've been developing new capabilities to drive more satisfied participants, as well as give you confidence that **your program is keeping pace with anything else available in the market today.** As you consider your renewal with us, we wanted to let you know about two new services we think can have a tremendous impact on your goals. The first is a new weekly report that shows nonparticipants in the program how much benefit those*

who are participating are seeing in terms of their fitness and wellness, as well as how much they are saving, and benefiting in terms of healthcare, by being part of your plan versus the alternatives. This kind of communication on a monthly basis will provide a gentle nudge to help encourage them to get into the program for the great benefits.

Second, we've also added a new smartphone app with online tools, including automatic result tracking, and integration with popular fitness trackers. In tests, these touches have been shown to help your employees get more benefits from health and wellness programs, and feel like they're making progress on their goals. The result has been shown to be higher employee plan satisfaction.

6. **Anchor the price increase high and introduce "justified" discount.** *These new services and functionality will add approximately 8 percent to the annual cost of your plan. However, if you renew before the end of the month, we will reduce the price increase by 50 percent, making it just a 4 percent overall increase to get this level of service. You're making great progress. Stick with our program for another two years, and I know you'll get to your 80 percent participation goal and further increase your employee retention rates.*

As you see, this model closely follows the first five steps of the Why Stay message framework. Note also how the bolded text in the "Detail competitive advances" step describes new capabilities as keeping pace with the market, rather than disrupting the status quo, and ties them directly to the customer's original goal of increased participation. By framing competitive advances in this way, rather than as new and cutting edge, you're able to demonstrate you're staying current with the market without undercutting your own Incumbent Advantage.

Now you know how to keep your customers buying, and potentially paying more for, their existing solution: Reinforce Status Quo Bias and, whatever you do, don't disrupt yourself.

But what happens when you *do* need to disrupt yourself? What happens when you need to move your customer off the solution . . . but not away from your company?

That hybrid message is what you're going to learn about next.

6

Messaging for the Upsell

The Why Evolve Conversation

The chapters you've read thus far have validated one key idea: Your customer conversations cannot be "one size fits all." Different buying scenarios have different psychologies and thus require different messages.

But there's still a gap. And it's a big one. Because if you're like most organizations, you don't want to keep selling the same thing to the same customers over and over, even if you are able to get them to pay more for it. Eventually, you're going to want to sell them new stuff. Better stuff. Higher-value stuff.

That's the "Why Evolve" moment. And by their own admission, companies are mishandling it in a big way.

WHAT'S AT STAKE IN A WHY EVOLVE CONVERSATION?

The vast majority of respondents to a Corporate Visions survey believe upselling clients to higher-value solutions is an absolutely critical part of their growth strategy: 87 percent of respondents told us the upsell is "important" or "very important" to their revenue and retention goals (Figure 6.1). Despite this, however, a smaller majority, nearly 60 percent, admit they're only "somewhat satisfied" or worse when it comes to the speed and rate at which they convert existing customers to new solutions (Figure 6.2).

How important is the customer migration/upsell conversation to your revenue success and ability to retain customers?

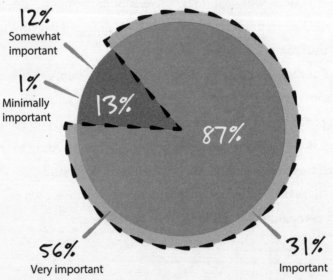

Figure 6.1 The majority agree: Upsell and add-on sales are important to companies' revenue and retention strategies . . .

How satisfied is your company with conversion rates of customers to your new solutions—in terms of both how fast they convert and how many are converting?

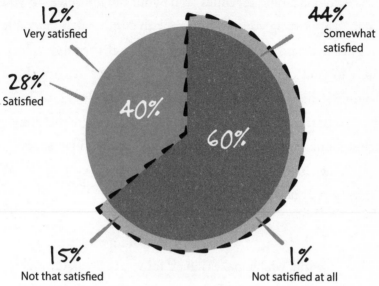

12%
Very satisfied

44%
Somewhat satisfied

28%
Satisfied

40%

60%

15%
Not that satisfied

1%
Not satisfied at all

Figure 6.2 ... but they're less than satisfied with their ability to convert existing customers to new solutions.

Convincing customers to migrate to a new solution should, theoretically, be easier than selling to brand-new prospects. Existing customers know you. You have a history together. They're more likely to pay attention to your marketing communications and meet with you to hear about your new offering.

But this conversation can go sideways on you without warning, surfacing hidden challenges and complexities that could scuttle any chance to forge that higher-value relationship, or even set the relationship back.

If you succeed at the Why Evolve conversation, you lay the groundwork for better customer experiences and longer-lasting relationships. If you stumble, these relationships stagnate. Just ask yourself how likely you are to achieve your annual goals if you only retain customers without growing your business with them.

And plateauing revenues aren't your only problem. If you aren't supporting your customers with continual, remarkable experiences and relevant solutions, they're all the more vulnerable to your competitors' disruptive messages. It's not about simply stalling out. It's about losing them entirely.

So before diving into the framework, it's worth taking a closer look at what can go wrong in this critical conversation.

A successful upsell message needs to answer each of the following five questions:

1. **Is it different enough?** Your customers live in a noisy world, which makes it hard for you to break through and be seen as different enough to compel action. And as you know from reading about Status Quo Bias, if everything looks similar, the safest course of action is to stay the same. So how do you create a message that's not what the customers expect—that's unusual enough to pique their interest?

2. **Is it important to their success?** To become the incumbent, you had to create a buying vision—that is, a vision of their future in which you and your solutions are pivotal to their success. Any new solution you propose needs to fit into that initial vision; otherwise, you risk disrupting yourself and undermining your Incumbent Advantage.

3. **Is it personally convincing?** Any message you create must not only show the value your new solution brings to their business but convince them to become personally invested in championing your cause.

4. **Does it incite change?** One of your advantages as the incumbent is that your customers see any change as a risk. So how do you get your customers to take the risk and prioritize the change without sacrificing that advantage?

5. **Does it drive purchase intent?** Ultimately, everything comes down to the purchase. Will they or won't they buy your solution? Even a small advantage can make a big difference. So how do you craft a message that gives you that critical edge?

Taken together, these questions present a conundrum: To address them all, you really need to answer two questions: "Why Change?" (the ideal customer acquisition framework) and "Why Stay?" (the winning retention framework). But you've heard throughout this book that introducing a change message to an existing customer is dangerous. You've also heard that the only way to change a customer's status quo is to disrupt it. That means you have to walk a delicate line between reinforcing the status quo and introducing just enough disruption to incite change. That's a tough proposition for even the most seasoned marketers and sellers.

This conversation is critical enough to your growth that it shouldn't be haphazard, based on guesswork, or built around some scientifically unproven formula. It deserves a message based on the buyer psychology in the moment at hand.

In short, it needs its own message framework.

7

The Winning Why Evolve Message Framework

For the Why Evolve research, we continued our collaboration with Dr. Nick Lee of Warwick Business School. The mission: Develop a message framework that supports the effort to sell upgraded or add-on solutions and services to existing customers.

Here's how we set it up:

At the outset, participants were randomly assigned to one of five test conditions. They were then told to imagine they were the decision maker in a discussion with a sales representative from their longstanding software vendor. The rep is trying to convince them to upgrade from a legacy, on-premise version of their business intelligence software to their new cloud-based business analytics solution.

The five conditions reflected the following message types:

1. **Product as Hero.** This is the model many companies use to announce new solutions. It's product-oriented,

focusing heavily on new and improved features and benefits.

2. **Why Change.** This message is provocative and edgy and has already proved effective in unseating an incumbent and converting prospects to customers. But would it work in a Why Evolve scenario?

3. **Why Stay.** Our previous research proved this message is most effective in convincing existing customers to renew at the *end* of a contract. But how would it hold up in the middle of the contract when an upsell is hanging in the balance?

4. **Relationship Reinforcement and Emotion.** This "hybrid" of Why Change and Why Stay uses strong emotional language to emphasize the partnership between the customer and the vendor, while at the same time initiating a frank conversation about shared challenges and opportunities.

5. **Social Influence.** This message deploys peer pressure as a powerful motivator, attempting to show the buyers that many of their peers are taking these same actions and they can't afford to be left behind.

As in our other experiments, participants experienced only one of the five conditions. Afterward, they were asked to respond with numerical scores to a series of questions aligned to the five key challenges outlined in the previous chapter. The responses were then averaged to form a composite index for each assessed area.

WHY EVOLVE: THE RESULTS

In a combined score reflecting the overall performance of each message across all positive areas assessed in the study, the message that performed best was Scenario #4: The hybrid "Relationship Reinforcement and Emotion" condition. This message outperformed the others by a range of 4.3–5.8 percent (Figure 7.1).

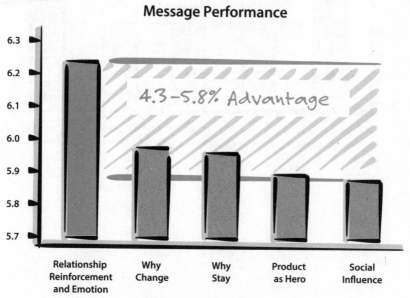

Figure 7.1 The hybrid Relationship Reinforcement and Emotion message carried the day—outperforming the others by up to 5.8 percent.

We also explored how well each message answered the five critical questions detailed in Chapter 6. Once again, the Relationship Reinforcement and Emotion condition outperformed the others across all five areas—in this case, by an even more significant effect size (Figures 7.2–7.6).

How important does this decision seem to your success?

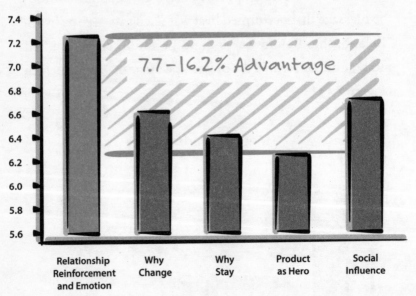

Figure 7.2

How willing are you to move to the new software?

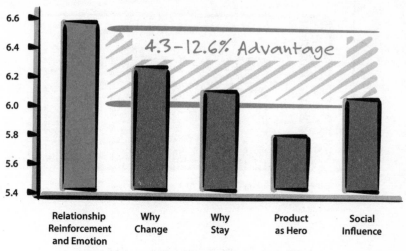

Figure 7.3

How likely are you to purchase the new software?

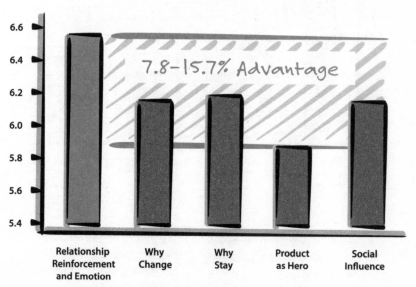

Figure 7.4

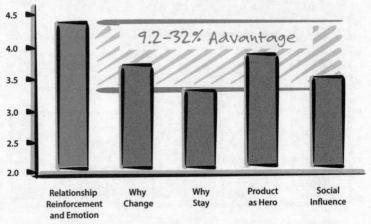

Figure 7.5

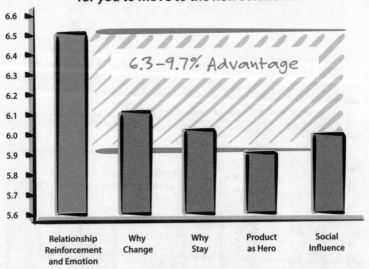

Figure 7.6

Figures 7.2–7.6 The Relationship Reinforcement and Emotion condition outperformed all other conditions across the five critical areas tested—importance to success, willingness to move to new software, likelihood to purchase, unusualness or unexpectedness of pitch, and convincing case to purchase.

It's worth calling out the poor performance of the "Product as Hero" condition, which underperformed all other conditions in several key categories, including "willingness to move to the new software" and "likelihood to purchase the new software"—in other words, the very actions a Why Evolve message is supposed to drive.

It's all the more puzzling, because as noted in Chapter 6, this is the preferred approach for many companies seeking to upgrade their customers. They lean heavily into the product message, assuming that the appeal of the "new" is enough to entice customers to buy more.

But think about this for a moment. Experienced marketers and sellers have long known that buyers hate straight product pitches, and they should know better than to deliver them. Yet for some reason, when it comes to positioning upgrades, all that wisdom goes right out the window—they are perfectly comfortable positioning the new capabilities as the main reason the customer should make the change. In fact, sellers often dress up the pitch as a favor to the customer: "I just went through some training on our latest solution, and I immediately thought of you. I think it would be a great fit in your environment, and I would love to talk to you about it."

It's great that you are thinking about your customers. They might be flattered that you thought of them. And they might even be impressed with your long list of cool features. But until you put those features into the proper context—by framing their needs within the right message choreography—they're simply not going to care enough to move.

THE WINNING MESSAGE: THE "HYBRID" (RELATIONSHIP REINFORCEMENT AND EMOTION)

The Relationship Reinforcement and Emotion condition (Figure 7.7) performed best in the study.

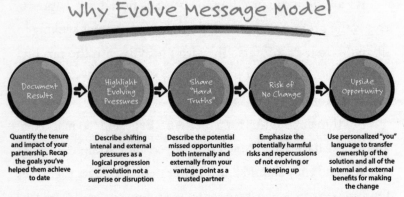

Figure 7.7 Use the Why Evolve message model to sell upgraded or add-on solutions and services to existing customers.

Here's the winning message, along with our analysis of why each element performed the way it did.

1. **Document results.** *Over our nine-year partnership, we have worked together toward your goals of creating organizational efficiency, increasing customer satisfaction, and protecting and growing revenue.*

   As with the Why Stay message framework, the most effective opening move is to reinforce the relationship by showing all the great things you and your customers have done together. And just as in Why Stay, some underperformance is okay as long as you're showing some progress toward the customers' goals and not simply focusing on the metrics you performed best on.

2. **Highlight evolving pressures.** *As with anything else, business needs change and technologies evolve. Externally you face a customer base that wants personalized solutions and instant answers. Internally you have a changing workforce that wants the newest tools and greater work flexibility.*

    This is where you see the first signs of the hybrid message. You want to raise the idea of change; otherwise, there's no reason for the customers to do anything different. At the same time, you don't want to introduce anything so radical it would drive them to investigate other options. Describing the evolving pressures as a logical progression of their current state creates just enough disruption without sacrificing your Incumbent Advantage.

3. **Share "hard truths."** *As partners, it's tempting just to focus on all the positives, but the role of a good partner is to also share hard truths. The fact is, we've heard from your teams that they like our software, but they are frustrated at having to dedicate time consolidating data from different sources. Then once the data is consolidated in your system, they feel limited because your current version has a limited set of standard reporting views available.*

    This is the most delicate step in the Why Evolve conversation, but it's also the most critical. Hard truths are the gaps and shortfalls in your customer's current approach—the approach *you* helped construct. It takes a lot of transparency and some vulnerability to reveal this to the customer, but that's also what makes it so powerful. When you are part of the status quo, you can't just tell your clients they're falling behind and are on a quick road to irrelevance. What you can do, however, is point to the emerging trends you discussed in the previous step and acknowledge where your solution falls short. Of course, you know your new solution will help close those gaps.

4. **Emphasize risk of no change.** *These areas of inefficiency can make it difficult for your hardworking teams to identify areas of waste, which means the organization continues to waste time. Not only does this make your employees frustrated and dissatisfied, but it can lead to clients becoming irritated that they aren't getting the personalized information and immediate experiences they desperately crave. This frustration has the potential to lead to more employee turnover and less customer loyalty.*

   Risk is a powerful human motivator. As you saw in Chapter 1, people are two to three times more likely to change to avoid loss than to achieve a gain, so any new message you deliver must contain a frank explanation of the risk your customer faces, as opposed to a litany of benefits. The balancing act is that you have to present this risk in a way that won't make your customers feel that you as a vendor are the source of the risk.

5. **Describe upside opportunity.** *But you can ensure your team has the latest version of the software that is so critical to your business. By upgrading to our new cloud-based solution, you'll get faster, simpler, and more flexible business management capabilities that allow you to acquire and analyze multiple data sources easily from a single app. You'll also tap into the power of artificial intelligence and be able to produce more than 50 standard reports that can be customized to your business. All this to improve the speed of your operations, the usefulness of your insights, while increasing both internal team and external customer satisfaction.*

In good messaging, you can't just tell people what they *shouldn't* do; you also need to give them a strategy for what they *should* do. Show them what their world will be like by helping them envision themselves using your solution and being successful with it. In this choreography, your solution is simply the means to that end. If the message is done right, this should not feel like a revolutionary change from their current state, but more a logical evolutionary next step.

One interesting result from this study came when we asked the question, "How likely are you to stick with your current solution?" It came as little surprise that the Why Stay story proved the most effective message type (Figure 7.8).

This is consistent with previous research into customer renewals and price increases, which found that reinforcing Status Quo Bias—as opposed to introducing new or provocative information—is the optimal approach for convincing existing customers to stick with what they have.

Likelihood of staying with current solution

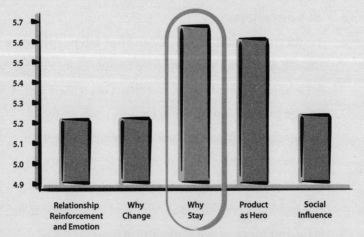

Figure 7.8 Reinforcing Status Quo Bias once again proves to be the most effective approach for convincing customers to stick with their current solution.

That a Why Stay message was once again effective at getting customers to stick with their current solution further validates the power of this framework for the customer renewal conversation—if your goal is to get the customer to keep buying the same solution. However, if your goal is to upsell or upgrade the customer, you need a message specifically designed for the Why Evolve moment.

The consistently strong performance of the hybrid message framework across all meaningful areas confirmed our hypothesis that the upsell moment calls for a different type of message than either the provocative Why Change or the protectionist Why Stay model. It's neither a straight acquisition nor a status quo reinforcement message; rather, it combines elements of each to exploit your Incumbent Advantage while still making the case for change.

This makes sense when you consider that the goal of this message isn't to drive a big change, nor is it about getting the customers to renew an existing solution. It's about getting the customers to *evolve*—to embrace change, but only as a logical progression of their ongoing pursuit of their goals. This "controlled change" messaging ensures they won't stagnate, but will instead embrace your innovations with confidence and enthusiasm.

⇒ 8 ⇐

"Sorry" Shouldn't
Be the Hardest Word

Apology Science and
the Expansion Sale

Whether you're in a Why Stay, a Why Pay More, or a Why Evolve conversation, you now know the importance of documenting results. When you're able to point to specific performance gains that are directly related to the customers' original goals, you reinforce their Status Quo Bias and capitalize on your Incumbent Advantage.

But what if the relationship hasn't been so perfect? And what if you're the one who screwed things up?

If you've been in business for any length of time, you've undoubtedly experienced that gut-wrenching moment when you realize something has gone terribly, terribly wrong. The network goes down. An order is bungled. A product has to be recalled.

Whatever the scenario, both the way you handle that failure and the conversations you have along the way are key to managing your customer's feelings about you later in the relationship. In fact, handling a customer crisis the right way can not only rescue the relationship; it can advance it to an even higher level.

It's a scientific theory called the Service Recovery Paradox, or SRP, in which your customers think more highly of you after you've corrected a problem than if they'd never had the problem to begin with (Figure 8.1). You've likely experienced this yourself, even if you didn't know the name for it.

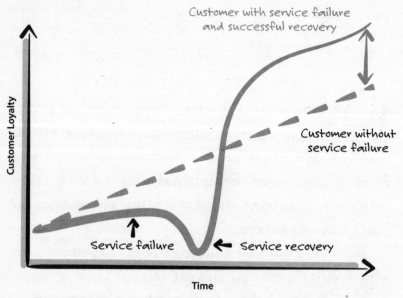

Figure 8.1 The Service Recovery Paradox is a situation in which customers think more highly of you after you've corrected a problem than if they'd never had the problem to begin with.

Think about the last flight delay you suffered through. If the situation was chaotic, communication was confusing or contradictory, or the gate agents treated you disdainfully, you likely came away from the experience vowing to avoid that airline in the future. But if you received timely updates, were compensated with food vouchers and bonus miles, and the gate agents were apologetic and empathetic, you probably would have thought, "Well, they did the best they could under the circumstances, and everyone was very professional." You might even tell others how well they responded.

That's the Service Recovery Paradox in action. But to maximize its benefits, you have to handle both the failure and its aftermath properly—including the apology conversation.

DO APOLOGIES MATTER?

It would be nice to believe every customer relationship is perfect, or at least not overly problematic. Even our own test simulations assumed the vendor achieved 50 percent of the customer's stated goals.

For some companies, that might seem like a pretty low bar. For others, however, that can seem like an insurmountable hurdle, especially if the implementation got off to a rocky start. Whatever the scenario, it's pretty much a given that at some point in the relationship, you're going to have to figure out a way to say "I'm sorry." So getting it right seems like it should be a pretty important conversation.

Most organizations concur.

More than 78 percent of respondents to a Corporate Visions survey agreed that apologies are very important, and that their customer retention rates and revenue growth absolutely depend on delivering a convincing apology (Figure 8.2). That came as no surprise to us.

How important to your company's success is your ability to apologize convincingly and effectively to your current customers when they experience a major product or service failure with your solution?

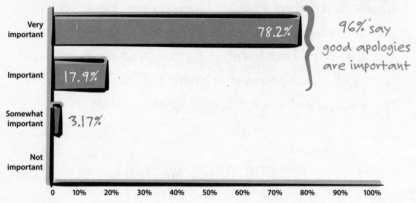

Figure 8.2 Survey findings showed that 96 percent of organizations say good apologies are important . . .

What was surprising was how ill prepared these same respondents were when it came to actually delivering apologies (Figure 8.3). Only 13 percent said they have a highly formalized approach with a documented structure that everyone knows and uses. Almost half—44.5 percent—take an ad hoc approach. And nearly 10 percent admit to simply "winging it," that is, letting individual account owners figure out how to handle this difficult conversation.

No wonder 82 percent of survey respondents feel less than "completely confident" in the effectiveness of their apologies (Figure 8.4). If they are achieving the Service Recovery Paradox, it seems like they're doing so purely by accident.

How formal is your process for apologizing to clients for major product service failures they experience with your solutions?

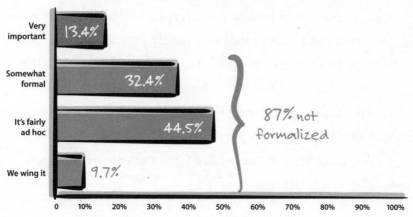

Figure 8.3 ... and yet only 13 percent have a formal process for handling apologies.

How confident are you in the effectiveness of customer apologies after a major product service failure they experience with your solution?

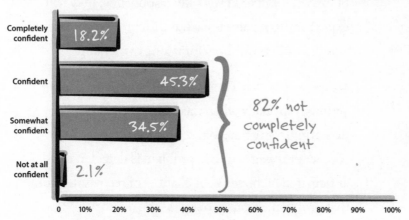

Figure 8.4 The lack of a formal apology process, combined with the criticality of the apology itself, could be one reason only 18 percent of companies are "completely confident" in their apologies' effectiveness.

A PARADOX EXPLAINED

The idea that a well-executed recovery can enhance your business has been documented extensively in B2C settings but never really examined in the B2B world. That changed in 2018 when the *Journal of Business & Industrial Marketing* published a study validating the Service Recovery Paradox in a B2B environment.*

The study set out four key components necessary to trigger the SRP in this setting:

1. **Initiation.** Willingness to engage in recovery actions, even if the problem wasn't caused directly by that provider, but rather by a subcontractor or other third party. In other words, even if the failure wasn't your fault, the customers don't want to hear you passing the buck. They will hold *you* fully responsible, they will expect *you* to resolve the issue with professional rigor, and they will reward *you* for taking ownership.

2. **Response speed.** Timely and responsive recovery actions, especially when the failure creates costly downtime for the customer. Taking immediate recovery measures once a problem is detected or anticipated increases your chances of recovering from that problem, versus providers who do not.

---

* Denis Hübner, Stephan Wagner, and Stefan Kurpjuweit, "The Service Recovery Paradox in B2B Relationships," *Journal of Business & Industrial Marketing*, February 2018.

3. **Compensation.** Allocation of physical and financial resources. While the B2B customers cannot typically pass the cost of the failure onto the provider, they will want some sort of compensation for the failure. That doesn't mean you have to fully refund purchases or make lots of giveaways, but they do expect you to provide additional free resources to resolve the service failure as quickly as possible. Delaying financial compensation doesn't elicit the same effect, nor does it restore your customers' trust. They expect you to resolve the problem immediately, at no cost to them, rather than make it up to them later.

4. **Apology.** Expression of remorse that conveys politeness, courtesy, and concern for the client. Your SRP will increase when you communicate your efforts to eliminate the root cause of a failure and convince the customer it won't happen again.

THE APOLOGY COMPONENT

While the first three of the above four components are essential to SRP, without the fourth—the apology—you can't document and communicate them. And without that ability, your customer won't appreciate or give you credit for your efforts, and your ability to achieve the SRP evaporates. It's also the one component that you, as the marketer or seller, can control. You might need to get approvals for compensation or escalations, but saying the right thing is free.

Because that ties directly to messaging effectiveness, that's the piece that piqued our interest.

For our foundational research on the apology component, we turned to a 2016 article called "An Exploration of the Structure of Effective Apologies" that identified the five specific steps a provider needs to take to apologize effectively:*

1. **Acknowledgment of Responsibility.** Demonstrate you understand your part in the service failure.

2. **Offer of Repair.** Describe how you're going to fix the problem and work toward rebuilding trust with your customer.

3. **Explanation of the Problem.** Explain the reasons for the failure.

4. **Expression of Regret.** Express how sorry you are for the problem.

5. **Declaration of Repentance.** Promise to not repeat the problem.

WHERE'S THE FRAMEWORK?

This seemed like a pretty comprehensive collection. But two things were missing.

---

* Roy Lewicki, Beth Polin, and Robert B. Lount, "An Exploration of the Structure of Effective Apologies," *Negotiation and Conflict Management Research*, May 2016.

First, in all our review of the existing apology science literature, nowhere did we find any guidance around sequencing. Does the order in which the provider executes these steps have a material effect on apology effectiveness?

Second, and of even more concern, what's the end game for the provider? While existing literature studies the general effectiveness of apologies, it doesn't examine the apology's impact on sales and marketing outcomes. What's the point of apologizing if it's not going to influence a customer's decision to continue to do business with you? Apologizing might make you feel good, but have you really accomplished anything if that customer feels good but doesn't continue to do business with you?

In short: There's no official, scientifically tested framework for developing and delivering a B2B apology.

That's what we set out to change.

9

The Winning Why Forgive Message Framework

Our interest in developing a scientifically proven message framework for apologies kicked off a broader research study with 500 participants across North America and Europe. With assistance from Dr. Nick Lee of Warwick Business School, we created a test scenario in which we asked participants to imagine themselves as a customer experiencing a service failure situation and measured their responses to important SRP-related questions.

The SRP only kicks in when the underlying service failure exceeds what researchers call the "zone of indifference"—meaning a failure that goes beyond the typical day-to-day missteps and token apologies common to most supplier-customer relationships. So we needed to concoct a scenario that ensured participants felt particularly acute pain that affected a wide range of stakeholders.

Here's what we presented:

Imagine you're the manager in charge of HR benefits.

Near the end of the benefits sign-up period, the software your employees use to sign up for benefits goes down for an extended period. Employees are e-mailing you directly with questions and frustrations, especially with the deadline looming. They are also submitting requests for support to IT, which cannot rectify the problem because it is an issue with the software supplier itself.

Your HR leadership team and other managers are repeatedly asking you for updates regarding when the problem will be corrected. The software ultimately comes back online, and the sign-up period ends. But this results in a much higher workload for you and your team to ensure all employees have the necessary benefits. You're also fielding numerous questions and concerns from company leaders worried about the impact this experience will have on employee satisfaction.

Once they read the service failure scenario, here's what we did next:

1. Asked participants to rank the intensity of their negative feelings toward the supplier in the story on a scale of 1 to 9, where 1 was the most extreme negative perception.

2. Pinpointed the angriest respondents—those who had rated their perceptions 1 or 2—as the subjects for the messaging test.

3. Drafted an apology that included each of the five components (steps) presented in Chapter 8.

Then participants were randomly assigned to one of five apology messaging conditions and were told:

> *You are about to meet with the software supplier for the first time since this serious incident put your department in such a difficult position. What follows will be the written text of the supplier's response to the situation.*

Finally, the participants read the apology as text and answered a series of questions. The responses from the most angry and frustrated participants (those who initially rated their perception of the supplier the lowest) were used to compare the impact of the various apology approaches. The objective was to determine which message could improve the reactions of the "saltiest" customers and provide a clear, winning formula to follow when you encounter a customer problem.

We drafted a sentence or two for each apology component. We then created multiple test conditions by reordering how the components appeared and were communicated to the customer, each defensible based on how effective any one apology component proved to be in the existing research.

Four different combinations of the five elements were created to test for the best approach. In addition, since a lot of people in B2B environments often eschew what they consider "sugarcoated content" and say they just want the straight facts, we created a fifth test condition as a control. This fifth condition contained only the two most factual apology components and eliminated the more emotional elements. We wanted to see how a factual account of the problem and description of the remedy would compare with the emotionally charged test messages. (See Figure 9.1.)

At first glance, you might not think that such subtle configuration changes, using elements already proved to be individually effective in previous apology science studies, would produce a single, consistent winning framework.

On the contrary, we discovered one of these approaches did outperform all the others across every question asked (remember, we were looking specifically at the responses of the most infuriated customer).

The one clear and consistent winner was test Condition #3 (see Figure 9.2). And despite what people say about not sugarcoating the message, the emotionless, just-the-facts approach consistently landed at or near the bottom on every question.

Condition #1	Condition #2	Condition #3	Condition #4	Condition #5
Acknowledgment of Responsibility	Offer of Repair	Offer of Repair	Expression of Regret	Explanation of Problem
Offer of Repair	Declaration of Repentance	Acknowledgment of Responsibility	Declaration of Repentance	Offer of Repair
Explanation of Problem	Acknowledgment of Responsibility	Declaration of Repentance	Explanation of Problem	
Expression of Regret	Expression of Regret	Explanation of Problem	Acknowledgment of Responsibility	
Declaration of Repentance	Explanation of Problem	Expression of Regret	Offer of Repair	

Figure 9.1 The simulation tested four different combinations of the five apology elements, with a straight, "just-the-facts" condition added as a control.

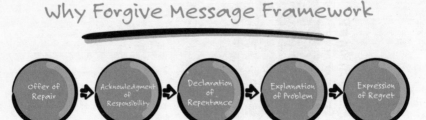

Why Forgive Message Framework

Offer of Repair → Acknowledgment of Responsibility → Declaration of Repentance → Explanation of Problem → Expression of Regret

Figure 9.2 Use the Why Forgive framework to increase customer satisfaction and loyalty, even after a service failure.

A CLEAR AND CONSISTENT WINNER

Looking at the questions best related to the Service Recovery Paradox, you will see that this winning approach measurably improves your ability to increase customer satisfaction and loyalty, even after a service failure. We didn't ask questions about satisfaction or loyalty directly, but instead asked behavioral outcome–type questions related to willingness to continue to buy from or buy more from the supplier. We also asked questions related to advocacy and willingness to recommend or serve as a reference for the supplier. All this was asked after "experiencing" the failure and reading the apology.

Compare this winning framework with what is usually passed on as the conventional wisdom for communicating a service failure in a B2B setting. It's almost a mirror image. Most people are told to say something like, "Here's what happened, here's what we're doing to fix it, we're very sorry this happened, it won't happen again, and here's what we'll do to make this right." But the winning framework looked nothing like this.

As Figures 9.3–9.6 show, Condition #3 is the clear, consistent winner. Meanwhile, there's so much variability in the other approaches, you can't even pick a clear second-place winner. This, despite the fact that the first four conditions all use the exact same content, just presented in a different order. This proves the power of story choreography. It's not just *what* you say, but *how and when* you say it.

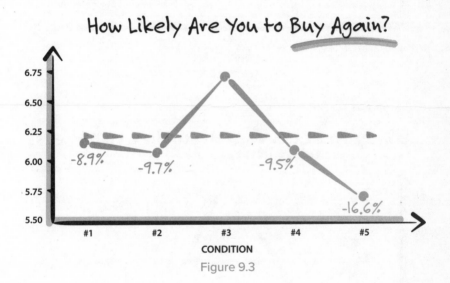

Figure 9.3

How Likely Are You to Buy More?

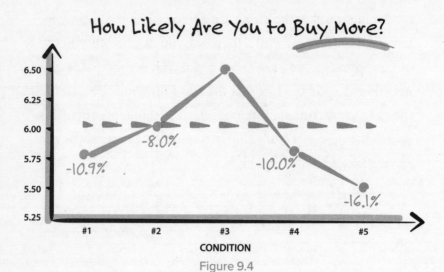

Figure 9.4

Likely to Recommend Supplier to Others?

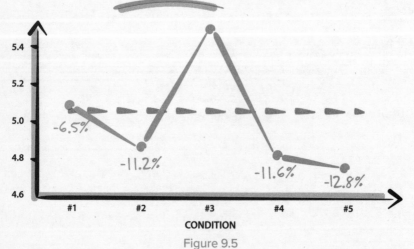

Figure 9.5

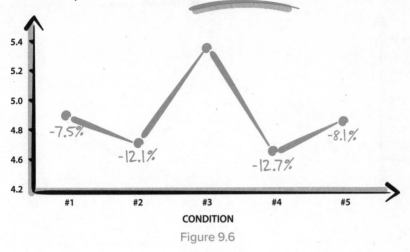

Figure 9.6

Figures 9.3– 9.6 The winning apology framework consistently outperformed all other conditions across key questions such as willingness to buy again, likelihood of buying more, and likeliness to recommend and refer supplier to others.

Another key indicator of apology success mentioned earlier is whether your customer believes that you fixed the problem and that the problem will not happen again. Even in this case, you'll see it's the same apology message that inspires the greatest confidence in the supplier moving forward—Condition #3. (See Figures 9.7 and 9.8.)

Confident They Fully Addressed Incident?

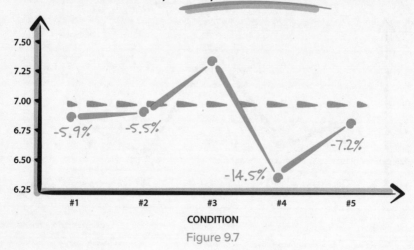

Figure 9.7

Convinced Incident Will Never Happen Again?

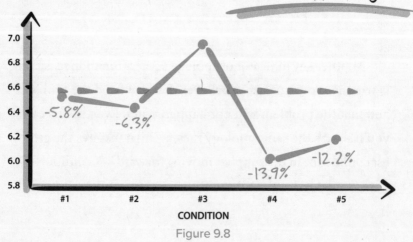

Figure 9.8

Figures 9.7–9.8 Using the winning Why Forgive framework increases customer confidence that the problem has been resolved and will not happen again.

A final set of questions and results was more tied to perceptions of the message itself, considerations such as the credibility
and overall effectiveness of the message. Once more, the clear
winner is Condition #3. Again—as you can see from Figures
9.9 to 9.12—due to the inconsistent results of the other messaging approaches, there is one clear winner and no clear second choice when it comes to the perceived quality of your
apology.

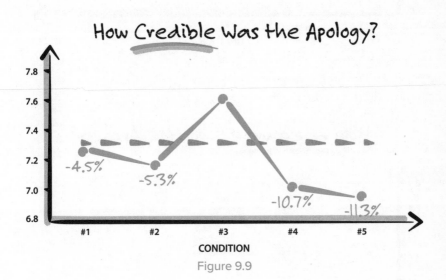

Figure 9.9

How Effective Was the Apology?

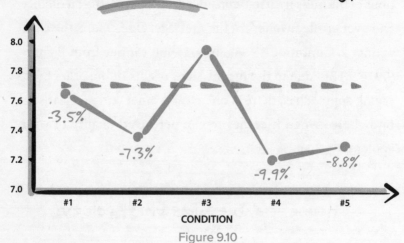

Figure 9.10

How Adequate Was the Apology?

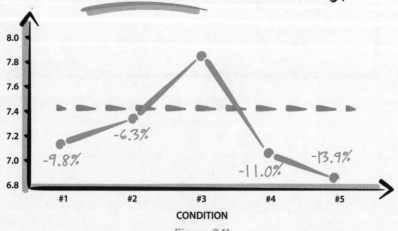

Figure 9.11

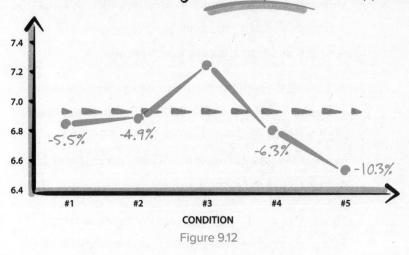

How Does It Change Perception of Supplier?

Figure 9.12

Figures 9.9–9.12 Using the winning apology framework boosts the credibility and perception of the supplier, and satisfies customers that the apology was both adequate and effective.

The Winning Example

Here is the winning apology messaging condition as delivered in the test:

1. **Offer of Repair.** *I want to attempt to repair any possible problems this outage caused for you, your team, or your employees. First, I have been approved to provide your company with a one-month refund, twice the length of your benefits sign-up period. It is an expanded refund in recognition that this happened at a peak time for your company. I have also directed our customer service team*

to manually check all sign-ups that occurred after the software came back online to be sure they were captured accurately. I will let you know the outcome as soon as it is complete, no longer than one week from now.

2. **Acknowledgment of Responsibility.** *The software outage was entirely our fault. It should not have happened at all, let alone during such a critical time for your business. We take full responsibility and are committed to ensuring it will not happen again.*

3. **Declaration of Repentance.** *I fully regret that this outage occurred, and our teams are making the necessary changes to make sure it does not happen again. Our outages should be reserved for planned downtime, with advance communication, and we regret that we failed on both accounts in this situation.*

4. **Explanation of Problem.** *To let you know what occurred, your software went down after a major power outage at one of our data centers. Your workload was rerouted to our other data centers, as part of our backup plan and service agreement. However, the second center your content was assigned to was down due to preventive maintenance and a hardware update. This caused your system to go down for a period as the system reconfigured to find the next alternative for your workload. We have now updated our redundancy system to avoid anything like this in the future.*

5. **Expression of Regret.** *I am exceptionally sorry for this outage, and as soon as I knew about it, I was in constant communication with our technical teams until it was resolved. On behalf of our company, I would like to apologize not only to you, but your leadership team and all affected employees.*

THE SCIENCE OF "SORRY"

So why *did* the winning condition win? What can we conclude from the findings? Decision Science offers some tantalizing theories.

One involves something called the "primacy/recency effect." This happens when items at the beginning ("primacy") and items at the end ("recency") of a list or string of information are more easily recalled than items that appear in the middle.

It makes sense if you put yourself in your customers' shoes: Tensions are high, and your customers aren't going to care about the "why" behind your actual apology until they know how you're going to make things right. So you don't want to squander their peak attention with a long-winded, self-serving excuse for a failure, because by the time you get around to actually solving their problem, you've already lost whatever residual goodwill they might have held onto.

Think of it this way: Imagine you had an experience at a restaurant that was so bad you asked to speak to the manager. Until the manager says she's going to comp your meal, you don't want to hear any explanation. In fact, if the manager starts explaining ("It's unusually busy . . . the server is new . . . they're short-staffed in the kitchen . . ."), you'll probably get more frustrated, not less.

Responding to an emotional situation with a rational explanation will backfire. You first need to lower the emotional temperature, and the Offer of Repair is the best way to do that.

But if it were simply a matter of leading with the fix, why did Condition #2 underperform? Remember, both Condition #2 and Condition #3 led with the Offer of Repair—yet it was Condition #3 that was the clear winner. That's where "recency" comes into play: Research shows that the most resonant part of a message is what the recipient hears last. It's the sincere Expression of Regret at the end that appears to have tipped the balance in favor of Condition #3.

The lack of an emotional element appears to have also factored into the consistent, miserable failure of the "just-the-facts" approach. If you recall the research on executive emotions outlined in Chapter 1, as well as the cadence of the Why Evolve message framework, you'll also recall how important the emotional component is to a compelling, persuasive message.

The lesson here? While you might be inclined to shy away from including a sincere emotional component in your apologies, the science shows you'd be making a big mistake. You'd be sacrificing the very component that makes the apology successful.

MAKE YOUR APOLOGIES WORK FOR YOU

Mistakes are inevitable. Lost business doesn't have to be. The Service Recovery Paradox demonstrates that a service failure could become an opportunity to increase customer satisfaction and loyalty to levels greater than if your customer never experienced a problem with you.

But how you engage your customer to achieve this result matters. In this chapter, you've seen there is a clear and consistent apology framework you can use to build and deliver your apology message—and positively influence even your angriest and most bitterly disappointed customers.

PART II

DELIVERING THE EXPANSION MESSAGE

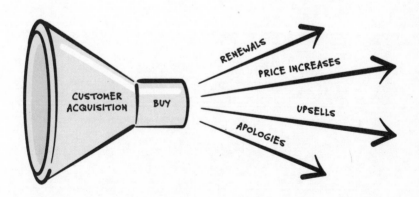

Now you know the science behind the four must-win commercial moments: You get your customers to buy again with Why Stay. You get them to pay more—and feel better about doing it— with Why Pay More. You upgrade them to a newer, better solution with Why Evolve. And for those times when the relationship couldn't get worse, you recover with Why Forgive.

You might think the science ends there. But if you're a marketer, seller, or customer success professional, that's just the beginning. Because now you have to *tell* the story. And not only do you need to make it memorable and persuasive, but you also have to know which story to tell at the right time—and through which channel.

That's what you'll learn about in this section.

⇒ 10 ⇐

The Right Message at the Right Time

Mastering Situational Fluency

One of our coauthors is an aspiring pilot. We wouldn't suggest going up with him quite yet, but his early experiences are a testament to the power and necessity of situational fluency.

In flying, context is everything. One of the first pieces of context an aspiring pilot must master is the different skills you need to execute takeoffs versus landings. During takeoff, you're primarily concerned with smoothly applying power, keeping the rudder aligned, and lifting off at the right speed. During a landing, you're managing power constantly—sometimes more, sometimes less—along with judging your descent speed and aligning with the runway. In short, while takeoff isn't easy, it's still a single set of inputs that yield a desired outcome. With landing, you're managing many more inputs, all of which require entirely different, in-the-moment decisions from the pilot.

Similarly, your company's revenue growth depends on your teams deciding which message to use at any given moment. As you saw, using the wrong message in an expansion sale can *actively undermine your ability to win more business* with an existing customer. Having the awareness of each unique customer situation, and applying the right message and skills in that moment, is what we call situational fluency. It's the ability to diagnose the customer situation, select the right message for that specific commercial moment, and execute that message with panache.

When we coach our clients on these skills, there's always a time when a participant will ask, "This all sounds great in theory, but how does this apply to my account right now?"

Our response is always, "Glad you asked!"

Here are the most common questions we hear from our clients, along with our responses.

WHEN DO WE REALLY BECOME THE STATUS QUO?

The key to situational fluency is recognizing which decision your customer needs to make so you can use the right conversation for that moment. Take the example of a new customer at the beginning of the customer's life cycle—let's call the customer Acme Corporation. At one time, it was an acquisition target. But luckily for everyone, your marketing and sales teams read *Conversations That Win the Complex Sale,* and now Acme is a customer. Congratulations! Now you're the status quo.

Or are you?

This is actually a time of great peril for your relationship. Your customer is coming from some other status quo. There are likely skeptics in the organization, including some who were involved in the decision to choose you. They could be waiting for your first misstep to find a reason to revert to the old supplier.

Even if everything is going swimmingly, the implementation will likely take time, which means Acme will incur costs up front while value trails. The solution might even need to coexist with the previous solution for some period of time, which increases your risk.

Not only that, but Acme is still two or three years away from a renewal conversation. And since Acme is just getting started with your current solution, there's nothing to evolve the customer to yet. Even your expected companywide price increase won't be hitting for another year—and because your implementation is going well, there's nothing to apologize for just yet.

It's tempting to conclude from all this that none of the four must-win commercial moments apply, and it's safe to take a deep breath, congratulate yourself on the big win, and move on to the next prospect. In fact, now is the ideal time to build your Incumbent Advantage and cement your solution as Acme's status quo.

You can do that by applying elements of the Why Stay framework:

- **Document results.** Start communicating results early and often. This sounds obvious, but remember the psychology behind it. Acme just decided to change, so early on there is a tension between the anxiety about whether the executives who made the decision made a bad choice (Anticipated Regret and Blame) and the desire to believe that they made the right one (Preference Stability). By sharing early results, you are showing that they did in fact make the right choice, and they can move past their anxiety. If your solutions are complex, and take time to show real strategic results, work with what you have. Even early, tactical results can show that you're on track to deliver the larger, long-term goals.

- **Review the prior decision process.** Early on, the actual decision process will still be fresh in the minds of the executives at Acme, so you don't have to rehash everything. But especially if it's too early to show strategic results, you want to reinforce that they made the right decision. Remind the Acme folks how your implementation plan connects to the big goals they wanted to achieve. For example, "Integrating this system will take some work, but it will eliminate the manual steps and potential failure point that was important during your evaluation."

The other steps—"Mention the risk of change," Highlight the cost of change," and "Detail competitive advances"—are less relevant early on. They'll become important later, but for now, focus on making sure that the company has fully transitioned to you as its status quo.

So much of this early-stage cementing of the status quo falls on the shoulders of your customer success team; yet there is plenty of room for marketing and sales to pitch in. Too many companies admit to poor handoffs between presale and post-sale organizations. Involving sales in these early customer success interactions can enable delivery of the very Why Change proposition that won the initial deal. Marketing can shift its messaging from disrupting to reinforcing, catching those second- and third-tier contacts at Acme that may not be directly involved in implementation or adoption, but may drive broader sentiment and advocacy across Acme's organization. A unified front can accelerate your solution as the new status quo—making that Status Quo Bias work for you much faster than your legacy competitor can possibly hold on.

WHEN CAN WE START THE WHY EVOLVE CONVERSATION?

With so many sellers needing to expand business to meet their quota, they're going to be naturally anxious to start the Why Evolve conversation. But when is the right time to begin that discussion?

The natural answer is, as soon as possible. And we would agree—in theory. Why not take advantage of the earliest opportunity to position your next big thing?

Think back to the different frameworks tested for the winning Why Evolve conversation. Compare the typical starting point for an expansion conversation with the message that ultimately won. Often the impetus for an expansion conversation is the flashy new product your company is bringing to market. Perhaps it's the latest upgrade or bundle that you know your customer would just adore. Or maybe you have a customer that's fallen behind and needs the new offering just to keep up.

And what's often the first instinct? Run to the product. Lead with the shiny new thing. The marketing collateral is top-notch, sellers receive product training at the annual kickoff, and customer success knows the intricacies of how it will fit in the customer ecosystem. But this approach loses—and loses by a lot. It's all about you, your company, your products. There are no customer stories in this approach. There's no reference to the stability of the relationship. It's "product as hero" or "social influence." It's ever so tempting to get caught up in the new and lose sight of the commercial outcome. Don't let it happen to you.

So in the spirit of situational awareness and with an eye toward increasing your chances of commercial success, here are two questions to consider before launching the conversation:

1. **Have you started delivering value?** Until you've started delivering some results, you haven't earned the right to start selling the next thing. You don't want to send the message to your customers that growing their spend is more important than their success. You also don't want to give them the impression that you intentionally underscoped the initial solution to get their business. You don't have to fully complete every goal you set before beginning the next conversation, but you do need to have some track record.

2. **Is the relationship stable?** Is there a service failure that needs correcting? If so, you need to execute your Why Forgive framework and make sure the relationship is on solid ground before you start asking for more. More broadly, however, stability might be hard to pinpoint, especially in situations where your customer is experiencing your solution every day, multiple times a day. The likelihood of a consistently positive experience, day in, day out, is slim—even for your best solution. There will always be glitches and detractors. So you need to establish a situational baseline for stability: When is the relationship strong enough for you to execute any revenue-generating conversation—a renewal, a price increase, or an upsell—and *not* get laughed out of the room for trying?

Answering no to either of these questions requires a pause. Until you've passed the "stories and stability" test, the relationship isn't ready for the expansion conversation.

That said, you don't want to wait too long either. If you wait for everything to be running perfectly, you'll never have that conversation. And as you learned earlier, if you wait too long to introduce new capabilities—that is, if you introduce them at the end of the contract term—you risk disrupting your customer at the wrong time. *Rule of thumb:* When you have some results to point to and the relationship is stable, it's safe to start the Why Evolve conversation.

WE MADE SOME IMPROVEMENTS, BUT THEY'RE NOT DRASTIC. IS THAT WHY STAY OR WHY EVOLVE?

This is a common question. The Why Stay framework doesn't mean you literally changed nothing about your solution. The "Detail competitive advances" step is where you describe what's new in a way that's not too disruptive. So how much change in your capabilities fits in that step of Why Stay, and when have you crossed over into Why Evolve territory?

You've read a lot of science in this book, but this nuance requires a little art. There's no way to test every permutation of new capabilities and compare all the frameworks. So think about this in terms of what you know from Decision Science. It's not about how much you want to sell to the customers; it's about what you're asking them to do. If your new capabilities mean they can do things more or less the same, but they can do them faster or better, then Why Stay is the right choice (for example, expanding the list of standard reports or dashboards). If you are asking them to change how they do things, then you're in Why Evolve territory.

WE'VE MADE MAJOR CHANGES. IS THAT WHY EVOLVE, OR DO I START OVER WITH WHY CHANGE?

Sometimes you really do have a breakthrough, something that will change the game for you and your customers, and it feels bigger than asking the customers to "evolve."

Do you ever have to completely start over and use the disruptive Why Change message? Remember the original Why Stay research. It showed that if you use a disruptive Why Change message, you give up your Incumbent Advantage and make it easier for your customers to switch. The psychology behind Why Evolve is to make a case for your customers to change, but without giving up your Incumbent Advantage. In almost all cases, you can propose significant changes within the Why Evolve framework. That's because most changes, even big ones, influence how your customers achieve their goals, but they don't change what those goals are. And that's the key test for Why Evolve. As long as you can connect your new capabilities to their existing goals, it fits.

Take the classic example of disruptive technology—the iPhone. If you sold telecommunications when the iPhone was introduced, did it really change your customers' business models? Not really. Before the iPhone, corporate IT departments gave their mobile workers flip phones so they could be productive. The goal of making mobile workers productive didn't change, but the definition of "productive" shifted. It evolved. Now they weren't limited to just making calls and returning voice mails while out of the office. They could e-mail, or they could access their CRM to be better prepared when they did return a customer's call.

As long as there is an existing relationship, and therefore an Incumbent Advantage, Why Evolve will be the better choice.

I WANT TO EXPAND INTO A NEW DIVISION OF AN EXISTING CUSTOMER. IS THAT WHY EVOLVE OR WHY CHANGE?

Sellers and marketers talk about upselling and cross-selling together; but through the lens of the status quo, they are different things. Upselling is selling more to the same customer contacts or stakeholder groups, which means that you are part of their status quo and have an Incumbent Advantage. Cross-selling means selling your solutions to new business units. You might have a relationship with the company, but that doesn't mean you have an Incumbent Advantage with that new buying center. If the new group you're targeting doesn't work with you, doesn't use your solutions, or doesn't benefit from the solutions directly, then you aren't part of that group's status quo. In this case, using you means the group has to change, and you need to use the Why Change framework. Your existing relationship still helps. You can get a warm introduction and/or a reference, but you still have to disrupt the unit's status quo. Putting the last two questions together, you can use a general rule of thumb:

- Selling the same things to the same people = Why Stay

- Selling new things to the same people = Why Evolve

- Selling new things to new people = Why Change

MY WHY EVOLVE UPSELL CONVERSATION DIDN'T GET TRACTION. WHAT DO I DO NOW?

Stability? Check. Stories with documented results? Check. Off to the races on that Why Evolve conversation. And yet sometimes that conversation doesn't work as you expected—often due to factors totally outside your control. Your customer is having a down year. Budgets got cut as new leaders came in. You're faced with the prospect of defending the slice of business you have or losing it altogether. And sometimes your Why Evolve message wasn't good enough to make the case.

Here's the cardinal error we often see from organizations when faced with this situation: They keep pursuing the upsell, missing the signals that it's time to switch gears to the renewal moment. And if the customer wants A, and all you present is A + B, then the possibility of C—moving away from you altogether—becomes more likely. Unwittingly, you can lose the Incumbent Advantage you've worked so hard to achieve, because you didn't demonstrate the all-important situational fluency.

We use a handy rule of thumb for customers we work with on Why Stay conversations. It's anchored by 75 percent. Companies are finding that if your customer hasn't decided to expand with you by the 75 *percent* mark of the initial contract term, it's time to refocus efforts entirely on Why Stay to retain that client. Getting the customer to buy again at this point is a victory.

Yes, there will be times when that feels like a step back. Yes, when your company's growth is predicated on the upsell, it will feel difficult to fully reinforce the status quo. Think of it less as losing out on the immediate expansion and more as delaying the future upside. Often, retaining that customer gives you more time and opportunity for the upsell conversation. You get the stability of an additional purchase. It may not be at the time you want, but it keeps the competition out and gives you greater incumbency to play with.

To be clear, reinforcing the status quo through the Why Stay conversation isn't just for those last-mile, save-the-business conversations. The best status quo reinforcement conversations underpin the full life cycle of the existing customer relationship. No piece of business is ever yours forever, and your competitors are never far behind. The Why Change message you used to win the business may have been fantastic; in fact, your competition is likely building a new one to displace you. If you're waiting until that renewal date to dive into all the wonderful things you've done together, you're too late.

WHEN DOES A SERVICE FAILURE RISE TO THE LEVEL OF NEEDING THE WHY FORGIVE (APOLOGY) CONVERSATION?

There's no shortage of think pieces on whether "sorry" is said so often in the workplace that it loses its effectiveness. Do a web search for "customer apology letter" and you'll get more templates than you have dissatisfied customers. Your challenge is to distinguish between those small service hiccups that don't impact the overall relationship and those true failures that deserve the full Why Forgive treatment. And the relationship stability you need for those retention and expansion commercial moments only exists in the former.

When you read about the winning Why Forgive framework, you might have noticed a concept called the "zone of indifference" that's immensely helpful to discerning relationship stability. It encompasses the type of failure where your off-the-cuff "I'm sorry" will likely do the trick—a small problem, confined to a single customer stakeholder, that you solve quickly with limited need for follow-up. The customer basically shrugs and moves on.

But once you get outside that zone—look out and have your winning apology ready. Outside that zone, stability is an illusion. The problem becomes a crisis, a true service failure. It doesn't just affect one person; it affects entire teams. It cuts across the customer's business in a way that's getting all the wrong attention. That's your Why Forgive moment—and that's when you know that your first goal is stability and relationship repair. Normally, these situations aren't difficult to diagnose— angry customers are tough to ignore—but that's when executing on the winning formula is so important.

THE RIGHT MESSAGE FOR THE MOMENT

As you read this chapter, there were probably other customer scenarios that came to mind that raise the question, "Which message do I use here?" No matter how many scenarios we address in this chapter, there will always be more that we left out. That's because every customer and every situation will be a little different. Good selling and marketing will always require good judgment and situational fluency, and a few simple principles can help clarify your thinking.

Two of the topics covered in this book are event driven and pretty straightforward: If you have a service failure, use the Why Forgive framework, and if you have a mandatory price increase for an existing offering, use Why Pay More.

For the others—Why Stay, Why Evolve, and Why Change—answer a few simple questions in regard to your customers. Are you currently part of their status quo? If yes, you can rule out Why Change. If you are trying to simply retain their business, and not asking them to change how they do things, Why Stay is most likely the right choice. If you are asking them to buy more, but more importantly *change how they do things within the context of your existing relationship*, then Why Evolve is the choice.

The good news is that each of these message frameworks is highly repeatable. Once you've identified the right framework to use for a given customer conversation, you can use it, with only minor tailoring, with other customers wrestling with the same decision. It will be worth it. The science says so, our original research says so, and the thousands of marketers and sellers who use these frameworks and see the results say so.

⇒ 11 ⇐

Delivering the Message

Essential Skills
for the Expansion Seller

Have you ever ordered something online, only to have the box arrive at your home dented and torn? You nervously peel back the tape and peek inside, hoping your item hasn't been damaged. And if it is, even if the manufacturer sends a replacement, all the initial excitement and enthusiasm around your initial purchase has dissipated. The entire experience falls flat.

The same concept applies to your customer conversations. You can construct a scientifically sound, persuasive message that you're excited about, but if you don't deliver it the right way, it loses much of its power. Just as you need different messages to connect with customers during these different commercial moments, you need to use different skills to communicate those messages.

The key is to execute these skills within the context of each message framework. Just as you need to apply the right message at the right moment, you also need to apply the most effective skill to communicate that specific element of the message.

DOCUMENTING RESULTS

Whether you're in a Why Stay, a Why Pay More, or a Why Evolve conversation, your first step remains the same: You need to document the results and successes the customer has achieved by working with you. That means first and foremost knowing your customers' goals. And not only knowing the goals, but how your customers measure their progress against them. Ultimately, you need to measure how your solution helped your customers get closer to (or achieve) those goals than they ever would have otherwise.

As noted earlier in this book, it might be difficult to get this information from your customers. Sometimes they don't track it consistently. Sometimes they won't want to share it. And too often, they simply don't know what the metrics are or where to go in their organizations to find them.

That's one of your earliest opportunities to start establishing your Incumbent Advantage. If your customers truly don't know what to track or how to track it, why not tell them? Sit down with them during the sales process and help them determine what success will look like for them and develop a mechanism for tracking it. After all, you've sold your solution many more times than your customers have purchased it. Who better to advise them on what they should expect?

One helpful framework for documenting results is something we call the "Triple Metric" (Figure 11.1). Using this framework helps ensure you're tracking results that are meaningful to the person you're meeting with but that also link to results your senior-most customer stakeholder cares about, on three levels:

- **Corporate.** How will your solution support your customer's highest-level performance measurements—the goals you might find in your customer's management presentation or shareholder letter? Think of measures like increases in revenue or improved cash flow.

- **Business Unit.** How will your solution help your customer create business or operational change at the department level, and how do those changes then ladder up to the "corporate" metrics? Metrics such as productivity, employee engagement, or win rates will be critical here.

- **Project.** How will your solution help your customer achieve the tactical changes necessary to support the overall goals of the department? These are the metrics most sales and customer success teams know and love—completing projects on time and on budget and meeting service-level agreements.

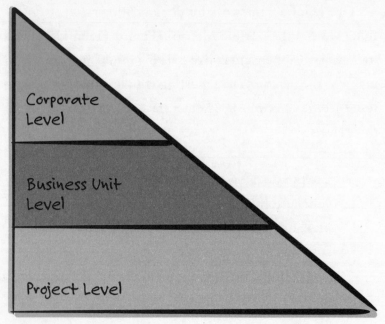

Figure 11.1. Use the Triple Metric to ensure you're tracking results that are meaningful to the person you're meeting with, as well as to the broader organization.

The key here is to collaborate with your prospects during the initial sale to identify their desired outcomes and come up with meaningful, yet achievable measurement criteria. And even if you didn't own the initial sale, or the customers bought without a clear measure of how your solution could impact those corporate goals, there's no time like the present to start identifying those key outcomes in collaboration with your customers.

As you start documenting results for your expansion conversation, begin with the challenges they were trying to solve when they first started talking to you. What goals did they talk about? When completing this step, make sure you include these three points:

- What was their previous situation? How were they operating before they purchased your solution?

- What were they able to "do" differently as a result of your solution? Here you want to document concrete actions they were able to take, such as changes in specific processes.

- What did that "mean" to them from a financial or business impact perspective? In other words, what was the value they achieved? The closer that value is to what your senior buyers care about, the better.

And that's often the biggest challenge for expansion sellers and customer success teams—elevating customer value back up to the most senior stakeholders that signed off on the initial purchase. There is immense comfort of day-to-day metrics and reporting at the project level of the Triple Metric. You probably have a customer scorecard or dashboard, a monthly status meeting, or a project update forum. Look hard at the measures that you bring to those meetings. How many are about how *your* company is performing? How many are about what *your* company has achieved? Documenting that you've hit *your* 99.8 percent uptime SLA or that *your* trains are running on time (for lack of a better cliché) does little, if anything, to prove what your customers are doing differently because of your solution.

That's where the connective tissue of the Triple Metric must come into play. Don't get us wrong—you'll often need to report those project-level metrics. It's likely baked into your contract.

Your job in documenting results is to link those project metrics to department outcomes and ultimately to corporate goals. If that connection doesn't exist or is unclear to your customers, your results lose power. The more your conversations anchor on corporate goals, with verifiable outcomes against those goals, you won't merely start your message successfully. You'll keep the ongoing attention of the senior buyers that will need to sign off on that renewal, price increase, or expansion sale.

Once you've collected all the information and made those connection points, your next step is to bring it to life in your conversation. That means framing the results in a way that grabs and holds your customers' attention. There are a few ways to do this, but when you're documenting results, the two most effective ways are through techniques called Number Plays and Customer Stories with Contrast.

1. **Number Plays.** This technique involves sharing a series of numbers (usually three) that build into a single story. The most effective Number Plays share information the customers didn't already know— or create a new insight they had not previously considered.

   When developing a Number Play, first identify the main point you want to make. For example, if you want to draw attention to cost reduction over time, you might want to use numbers to represent the amount of time they've worked with you, the percentage decrease in costs over that period, and the hard dollar savings they've realized.

Number Plays are best delivered in writing, on a flip chart or whiteboard. If you happen to be meeting with your customers over the phone or the web, try having them write the numbers as you dictate. In either case, share the numbers first—just the numbers, with no indication of what they represent. Then, as you tell the story, fill in the labels to build the story:

> *22, 12, and 4. <WRITE numbers> These numbers tell a story. Reducing costs is often painful, but not in this case. In the 22 months <WRITE "Months"> you've partnered with us, you've been able to measure a 12 percent <WRITE "%"> reduction in electricity use. This reduction translates into direct savings of over 4 million. <WRITE "Million" and DRAW country-relevant currency sign>*
>
> *Cost reduction efforts are more successful when everyone gets the mandate and the objective is broader than just next quarter's earnings. Making a strong case to all stakeholders—nationally, internationally, and with your union workforces—requires you to convey urgency and criticality.*
>
> *These initial results make the case to evolve further, and that's what you're going to hear about today: how to get everyone aligned around further reducing your third-highest cost line-item—energy.*

Tip: Don't quiz your customers by asking them if they know what the numbers mean after you write them. They won't—and asking will only frustrate them. And if they can guess, you don't have an attention-grabbing Number Play.

2. **Customer Stories with Contrast.** Another way to bring your results to life is to create contrast in the minds of your customers by sharing a "before and after" story about the impact your solution has had on their business. By creating contrast between these two conditions, you establish the perception of value for your customers—and make it concrete and easy for them to understand.

   a. First choose the three key statistics from the Corporate or Business Unit level(s) of the Triple Metric that show the greatest value your customer has received by working with you (efficiency gains, reduction in costs, increase in accuracy, reduction in manual interventions, increase in throughput, or similar metrics).

   b. Next compare these to the customer's numbers from before they started working with you. For many companies this information does not exist. If you are in this group, you might want to think about implementing a process change to start collecting these key statistics for all new customers. To tell a story with contrast, you need to show where they were historically versus where they are today. The key is to show the journey they've taken and all the positive momentum that has been built up.

c. Finally, identify what changed in the customer's environment that led to these results.

Ultimately, your story might sound something like this:

Two years ago, when you first partnered with us, you were concerned about rising costs and declining quality. At the time, you were experiencing:

- *200 hours per quarter of unexpected downtime*

- *$1.5 million in annual unplanned overtime pay*

- *11.2 percent defect rate*

You can remember how painful that was, and how it forced you to cut investment in R&D at a time when your major competitors were launching new products every quarter. And that's why you came to us in the first place—because you knew that if you wanted to stay competitive, you needed to make a change.

Luckily, that change has paid off. Since implementing our solution, you've been able to reduce those numbers to:

- *10 hours per quarter of unexpected downtime*

- *$12,000 in annual unplanned overtime pay*

- *2.1 percent defect rate*

These improvements have gone directly to your bottom line, translating into savings of more than $2.5 million—which you've reinvested in a new product line that's scheduled for release in the spring.

Note the specificity in the above example, and how each bullet in the "before" scenario contrasts directly with the corresponding bullet in the "after" scenario. If you were to only focus on the latter scenario, the "after," you'd only be telling half the story—and you'd miss the opportunity to highlight the value your customer has realized.

It's also important to understand that "results" don't always mean "numbers." You can use both quantitative and qualitative metrics to document results. If you have no hard numbers to share, describe how their business is operating differently. Detail process changes your solution helped them implement. Use stories and anecdotes to illustrate their progress ("In our last conversation, you mentioned that employee engagement has gone up since we first started working together . . ."). This forces you to truly know your customer's organization and have ongoing conversations and interactions so you can pick up on individual successes and broader customer sentiment around your solution.

The more concrete your examples, the more your customers will see themselves in them.

VISUAL STORYTELLING FOR THE EXPANSION SALE

So you've learned how to share important information with your customers in a memorable way through Number Plays and Customer Stories with Contrast. But even those techniques might not be enough to ensure long-term retention of your message. In fact, research shows that only 1 hour after you share your message with customers, they'll only remember 50 percent of what you said. If that wasn't depressing enough, after 8 hours retention drops to 25 percent, and after 24 hours retention drops to only 10 percent. In other words, one day after you speak with someone, the person will have forgotten 90 percent of what you said. And you thought your customer was excited to talk with you!

A good way to see if this is a problem with your existing customers is to listen to the questions they ask during your follow-up calls and meetings. When you have these conversations, do you hear questions like, "Where did we leave off last time? Tell me again what the purpose of this meeting is? What were we talking about?"

Those of you in customer success are likely vigorously nodding along right now. Too often, that's how your typical monthly check-in calls begin. You're ready to share the latest adoption statistics, and your customer is asking what you talked about during the last call. It's once more an always-on fight between your message and your customer's brain.

How do you fight this forgetting cycle, where you share, your customer forgets, and then you share again? There's one scientific principle that will make you six times more memorable to your customer. The same principle will also help your customer remember your message six times longer. The principle is the "Picture Superiority Effect": When you combine your words with an image, your story will be more memorable.

And the good news is, the concept has been around for a while. Humans have communicated through pictures long before the spoken word, and yet too many customer conversations rely solely on the spoken word to convey critical business points. Even with the right message for the right commercial moment, without a complementary visual, marketers, sellers, and customer success teams are limiting their own effectiveness and squandering their most potent, built-in advantage.

Think of all the work that often precedes a single prospect meeting—marketing touches galore, cold calls, warm e-mails—all to get a seller one shot at delivering a compelling message.

The expansion meeting is a completely different ball game. You likely have standing appointments with your key customer contacts. You've scheduled quarterly business reviews with senior stakeholders at your largest accounts. You're having that always-on Why Stay conversation to reinforce the status quo. In other words, it's the ideal time to leverage the Picture Superiority Effect to solidify your Incumbent Advantage.

Do a quick comparison with your competitor, which desperately is trying to dislodge you. Let's say the people at your competitor haven't read this book, and don't use a visual in the one conversation they have. Your customer remembers little of the competitor's presentation. On your side, you ensure every standing meeting occurs. You prepare a simple visual for each one, often co-creating in the moment with your customer. Through visuals alone, you are exponentially building a competitive defense in your customer's mind. Your customer remembers more of your meetings, finds more value in your meetings, and thus takes and attends more meetings—and your status quo becomes firmer each time.

As you build your expansion visual, keep the following principles in mind (and refer to the examples in the Appendix for further inspiration):

1. **Paint a world in which your customers will see themselves.** If your visual doesn't resonate with your customers, it will not have the impact you need. You don't have to perfectly visualize their world, but it needs to be familiar enough that they can put themselves in the visual. Here your bar is high. Your customers expect a current partner to know this world. Visualizing it cleanly for them is an implicit signal that you "get it."

   In contrast, it cannot be your world. Avoid the temptation to portray your solutions. This is not a technical drawing showing how your solution specifically works. As wonderful as your offerings are, this isn't about you.

2. **Start with their thinking.** Envision how your customers see their world today. What problems and issues are top of mind? Now compare that with the contrast you need them to see. What's the difference? How can you visualize these two different states?

3. **Keep it simple.** Too many visuals overcomplicate the scenario. You're not creating an infographic—you're developing a memory tool to engage customers on a deeper level and help them remember and share your story more broadly across their organization. *A good rule of thumb:* If your customers saw your visual and heard you talk through it, could they retell that story three days later?

4. **Include contrast.** Recall that contrast is the key element to overcoming Selection Difficulty, and the best contrast shows the difference between loss and gain. Loss aversion continues to be your friend in your visual. When you include clear contrast in your visual, you make it much easier for the customers to make a decision. You can show the whole journey the customers need to take and increase the likelihood they'll follow your lead.

The contrast you demonstrate needs to differ based on the commercial moment that you're in. A

Why Stay visual will look different from a Why Evolve visual—and both will look different from a Why Change visual. This is exceptionally important for sellers with a book of business that spans all selling scenarios. As you read in earlier chapters, using the wrong message—and supporting it with the wrong visual—can ruin your opportunity for commercial success. For example, in a Why Stay visual, you want to show contrast between everything your customer has achieved and the risks or costs of doing something different. In a Why Evolve visual, you need to incorporate enough nuance to contrast the current approach, which to some degree is good, with the risks or costs of *not* making any change.

Tip: When you create a visual for your messages, try to avoid including too much exhaustive detail in your story. Focus on the elements that provide the greatest opportunities for sharp, memorable contrast:

- If you are creating a Why Stay visual, focus on these three questions:

  o How did you get to this point? (Documented results and prior decision process)

  o What's the risk of messing with success?

  o What's the advantage of staying the course?

- If you are creating a Why Evolve visual, focus on these four elements:

  o **Progress.** Visualize the progress that you've made together.

  o **Change.** How is your customer's environment changing and evolving?

  o **Reality.** What's the reality of the status quo? (Hard truths and risks)

  o **Opportunity.** What's the opportunity available to your customer?

  As Voltaire once said, "The best way to be boring is to leave nothing out." Use this as your mantra when you develop your visual story. That way, you'll ensure your story remains sharp, engaging, and, above all, memorable.

Picture superiority is a well-tested and well-documented science, but there was one big question associated with the concept: What type of picture is best? In storytelling, you have many ways to visualize your story, but which type is scientifically the most persuasive and effective?

This big question prompted original research conducted with Dr. Zakary Tormala, a professor at Stanford Graduate School of Business, who was contracted by Corporate Visions to conduct this experiment. The strategy in testing was to remove all variables except for the visual. Participants heard a single audio track with the same speaker saying the same words. While the talk track was identical, the visual they saw on the screen was different.

- One-third of participants saw a traditional PowerPoint slide with building bullets and a little stock photography.

- One-third of participants were presented with a whole screen image of a single picture with a few words on the page.

- One-third of participants saw a hand-drawn visual created on the screen.

In the testing, the hand-drawn visual won in all six categories tested (Figure 11.2). Of these, the credibility question was particularly interesting. The speaker in the hand-drawn condition was perceived as more credible than the others, even though everyone got the exact same message with the exact same audio track.

The feedback from the field reinforces these findings. People who adopt the hand-drawn visual approach will often say, "Customers are so much more engaged . . . It was the best meeting I ever had." From a customer perspective, comments are often "You really know your stuff" or "You've really shaped my thinking on this."

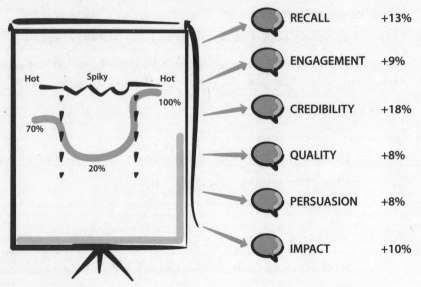

Figure 11.2 Use simple, concrete visuals to boost the credibility, memorability, and overall impact of your messages.

The goal is to have an authentic conversation with your customers, which means making it as organic and flexible as possible. This flexibility is important because it invites your customers into the conversation, and in a best-case scenario, they will pick up the pen and start "co-creating" with you.

But what happens if you're not in the room with them? That's a phenomenon that is increasingly common. In fact, according to statistics from InsideSales.com, 75 percent of all selling happens remotely. That includes the 50 percent of sellers who are purely inside, as well as outside sellers who are now conducting half of their sales conversations over the phone.

So how do you flex your powerful visual storytelling skills with a customer who's halfway around the world, linked to you only by a telephone?

According to a Corporate Visions study, adding an interactive visual to a remote sales conversation produced marked increases in message effectiveness, seller credibility, and information recall.

It makes sense. Think about the last time you heard something you really wanted to remember and understand. Did you just passively listen to the information and expect to retain it? Or did you jot down some notes and reminders?

The same principle holds true for your customers. Our research proved that getting your audience participating in some way—whether by taking notes or drawing a simple, concrete visual as directed—can give you an edge over less interactive approaches. You should be asking what participatory actions your audience can take to amplify and reinforce the story you're trying to tell.

Being More Compelling and Memorable in "Virtual" Sales Meetings

In collaboration with the *International Journal of Sales Transformation*, Corporate Visions worked with Dr. Nick Lee of Warwick Business School to develop a research simulation aimed at determining the most effective approach for being impactful in a phone or web conference selling environment.

The simulation, conducted online, involved 800 participants and tested a range of approaches, some more participatory and interactive than others. Specifically, the study was designed to assess the effect of these approaches on attitude/disposition and recall—two critical measures of effectiveness when it comes to engaging prospects in these environments.

The test simulation put four message conditions to the test in an inside-sales selling environment. At a basic level, the conditions included the following approaches:

- Listen Only

- Listen and Watch Only

- Listen, Watch, and Take Notes

- Listen and Draw as Directed

The first assessed area examined was attitude and disposition, to measure the effect on critical factors such as uniqueness, trusted advisor status, how compelling the call was, and how likely it was to produce a meeting. Across these areas, the Listen and Draw as Directed approach consistently performed the best.

The study also assessed the recall and retell-ability of the various conditions—both key indicators of how remarkable and memorable the call was. In this case, the Listen, Watch, and Take Notes condition was a convincing winner across areas like confidence in recall, number of correct recalls, and confidence in retelling the story to colleagues.

In a customer expansion environment, the ability to positively affect the attitude and recall of an individual customer could be a major boon as far as driving consensus among multiple decision makers. By inspiring an individual stakeholder, you increase your chances that the stakeholder will champion your story inside his or her organization and get other decision makers to rally around it. That's the kind of positive ripple effect across a buying team that all sellers want. By keeping the conversation more participatory (and more engaging and memorable), salespeople increase their odds of achieving that outcome.

OWNERSHIP VERSUS PARTNERSHIP IN THE EXPANSION SALE

A recurring theme runs through all the frameworks and techniques you've learned so far: *Don't make it about you.* Customers care about themselves first, so instead of fighting that fact, go with it and make your story about them.

One of the simplest, yet most powerful, ways to do this is through the language you choose. Using "you-phrasing"— that is, describing challenges and solutions in the second person, from the customer's perspective—can materially change the way your customers react to your expansion conversations. In many cases, doing this is merely a matter of changing the subject of the sentence from you and your solution to the customers and their results. For example, instead of saying, "*Our solution* reduced downtime at your plant by 10 percent," you can say, "*You've* reduced downtime at your plant by 10 percent." You'll immediately sound different from your competition, and you will elevate your value and level of trust in the minds of your customers. More importantly, you're assigning ownership to the customers—ownership of the challenge and risk, so they feel the emotional impact; and ownership of the solution, so they become the "hero."

In the classic book *The Hero with a Thousand Faces,* Joseph Campbell details the typical steps in the "hero's journey" throughout myth and stories around the world. While the journey is never easy, the role of the "hero" is still desirable. The other key role in Campbell's model is the "mentor." A mentor's job is to counsel and guide the hero in times of struggle.

The two scientific concepts underlying this premise are often referred to as "self-relevance" and "invoking imagination." Self-relevance is the tendency for people to recall information at a much higher rate when it's related to themselves. After all, who doesn't want to be the hero of his or her own story?

In an acquisition conversation, this concept is pretty straightforward. Everyone agrees that customers want to be the hero, and everyone also agrees that the supplier should be the mentor. In fact, when we share this concept with sellers and marketers, they all enthusiastically identify themselves as the mentor. Even though their websites, brochures, and pitch decks are still packed with "vendor-as-hero" language, hey, at least give them credit for having the right idea!

In an expansion conversation, the lines seem a bit blurrier. After all, you've just read through a series of message frameworks that urge you to reinforce your status quo as a trusted partner. Wouldn't that mean, therefore, that you and your customer are taking the hero's journey together, and that you should convey this through what we call the "inclusive we"—that is, using "we-phrased" statements that convey shared accountability for the challenges and joint ownership of the results? So in the example above, you'd say something like, "Through our partnership, we've reduced downtime 10 percent."

In fact, that's the primary engagement approach used by a plurality of respondents to a Corporate Visions survey on the topic. Although more than half (52 percent) of the companies we surveyed agreed that you-phrasing should generate better results, a slightly smaller percentage, 47 percent, admitted that they we-phrase their customer communications. What's more, they do so deliberately, believing it positions them as a trusted partner who brings value and insight to customers.

So are they right?

Not according to the science.

In fact, our research shows that you-phrased messages outperform the inclusive we-phrased messages across every major category tested. In our simulation, participants who received the you-phrased message were:

- 21 percent more likely to feel responsible for solving the problem

- 13 percent more likely to take action

- 9 percent more likely to feel the issue is important to the organization's future success

To see how these principles come together in a fully articulated expansion story, turn to the Appendix. Then use the planners provided to begin building your own messages.

⇒ 12 ⇐

Navigating
the Conversation

Advanced Skills
for the Expansion Seller

Okay, so you've mastered the fundamental skills you need to communicate your customer expansion story for maximum impact. You've learned how to use you-phrasing to make your customer the hero of the story. You've learned how to use visual storytelling to improve engagement and retention in both face-to-face and remote selling situations. And you've learned how to document results and present them to customers in a way that reinforces their Status Quo Bias.

But what about the rest of the conversation? What else do you need to know to make sure you're wringing every possible piece of value from each step in the framework?

Let's revisit the steps of the Why Stay, Why Pay More, and Why Evolve messages and examine additional ways to make your message more powerful.

NAVIGATING THE WHY STAY CONVERSATION

The Why Stay conversation is all about status quo reinforcement. It's not the place to introduce disruption, new ideas, or any startling information. At the same time, you want to avoid sounding defensive or frightened when discussing the risks and costs of change. That's why it's important to begin the conversation in your customer's world—with their goals and outcomes thus far—and keep the risk discussion measured and practical.

- **Step 1: Document results.** As you learned in previous chapters, your first step is to quantify the tenure and impact of your relationship. Do this by first revisiting the goals you and your customer established during the sales process. If you used the Triple Metric described in Chapter 11 to set these goals, you'll already have the framework in place and can simply report against that framework.

  Don't beat yourself up in this step if you haven't checked every box here. What you want to demonstrate in this step is not necessarily that you've helped your customer achieve all the objectives they set out to achieve. That's an unrealistic expectation. What you do want to show, however, is progress—that is, the contrast between where they began and where they are today. Demonstrate, using the delivery techniques you learned in Chapter 11, how they are on track to meet their objectives and highlight the positive outcomes they've seen thus far. Be sure to tie these outcomes back to the Corporate, Business Unit, and Project level goals you and your customer have already agreed on.

- **Step 2. Review the prior decision process.** Your next step is to revisit the original decision your customer made to work with you. You'll need to detail the following:

  - What did the process entail?

  - Who were the people involved, and who made the final decision?

  - What criteria did they use to make their selection?

  - Which competitors or alternatives did they consider and exclude, and why?

  - And finally—the big question—why did they ultimately choose you?

Now it's entirely possible the contacts you're dealing with on the renewal aren't the original decision makers and won't have any insight into the purchase history. That makes this discussion even more important, because that's information you might have that they don't. If you don't have that information either, you might be able to get it internally, through your customer success organization, your CRM database, or the seller who originally won the account. If the customer has been with you for a long time, remind him or her of that: "You've been a customer for eight years, and during those eight years you've had numerous opportunities to make a change. But each time, you looked at the options and came up with the same answer: sticking with us."

Work with what you have. And if all else fails, you can also try asking the customer. One of our clients didn't document any information about its customers' decision process, and because the client fielded a junior sales team with high turnover, it was impossible to find it. So someone from the sales team would simply say, "I wasn't here two years ago when you chose us. Can you tell me why you did? I know it wasn't because we were the low-cost provider, so what was it?" Not only did the customers answer the question; they often renewed their business on the spot because they reminded themselves of the value they'd been receiving!

- **Step 3. Mention the risk of change.** In this step, you are going to reinforce their Anticipated Regret and Blame by mentioning the risk of change. That means surfacing the business consequences of a bad decision—paying particular attention to risks that connect back to the goals you identified up front. This contrasts with the progress you've already documented for your customers and clearly puts their already-realized value on the line:

- ○ What's the impact on the business of going through another transition?

- ○ What makes this a particularly bad time to make a change?

- ○ What could go awry in the customers' world as a result of a failed change?

There are two important considerations here: First, you want to *mention* the risk—not hammer it home. It's easy to go overboard when warning your customers of the dire consequences of switching now, but if you lay on the fear, uncertainty, and doubt too heavily, you can come across as manipulative and unintentionally alienate your customer. Touch on the risk in a factual, empathetic way. Don't exaggerate! Your customer's Status Quo Bias will do that part for you.

Second—and this is going to feel uncomfortable—when we tell you to "mention" the risk, we mean "talk about it." Out loud.

Invariably, when we introduce this component in a workshop or presentation, someone will challenge us: "Are you seriously suggesting I mention changing providers to my customer? Why plant that seed? Why create a problem that doesn't exist?"

Our response is twofold. Our research showed that explicit mention, as shown above, was in the winning framework. It's inescapable. So the science supports this approach. Besides, do you really think that customers would never think of talking to a competitor until they get the idea from you? Of course your customers will talk to your competitors, whether you suggest it or not. Even if they aren't talking to competitors directly, they are seeing competitors' marketing materials, a sponsorship booth at a trade show, or that unsolicited LinkedIn message. And the risk of mentioning a switch that your customer hadn't thought about is minuscule compared with the risk of not mentioning it and sacrificing the power of risk aversion.

- **Step 4. Highlight the cost of change.** The next step speaks directly to the Status Quo Bias antecedent Perceived Cost of Change. Your customer already believes the status quo is free and switching carries a financial cost. But there are other nonmonetary costs to consider, such as lost time or loss of focus on current priorities. Choosing a new vendor isn't fast, and it isn't easy—it requires a lot of time and a lot of people.

  You might be in a situation where a competitor has offered a big discount to win your customer's business. Your job is to show the customer that any perceived savings will likely get swallowed up by the cost of change:

  - What's the cost of having to redesign processes?

  - How many people will need to be retrained, and how much per person?

Psychologist Daniel Kahneman won the Nobel Prize for his research on prospect theory, which focused on the role of risk and loss in decision making. In his experiments, Kahneman proved that people place at least two times as much value on avoiding a loss as they do on obtaining a gain. When you show your customers the risk and cost of change, you're deliberately focusing on the potential loss that they'll suffer if they move away from their status quo (you). So during your conversation, make sure to concentrate your questions on what your prospects stand to lose should they not renew with you (Figure 12.1). Prospect theory says you'll get a better response if you lead with the loss and then add the gain.

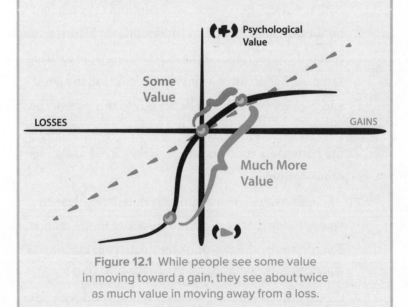

Figure 12.1 While people see some value in moving toward a gain, they see about twice as much value in moving away from a loss.

- How much time will it take to support users?

- What's the cost of reduced productivity, even if it's only temporary?

- **Step 5. Detail competitive advances.** The last step in your Why Stay conversation is the step where you get to talk about your stuff, the gain to contrast with the potential loss. At last! Only . . . not so fast. As you saw in earlier chapters, this step aligns with the Status Quo Bias of Selection Difficulty, in which a lack of contrast between competing alternatives negates any perception of value on the customer's part.

  Think about what this means. If your customers don't see any difference between your solution and the competition, their natural inclination is to stick with the status quo—you. So as excited as you might be about your new, unique, differentiated features, the renewal conversation is the exact wrong time to bring them up. Sellers attempting to shoehorn all the latest and greatest features and benefits into this part of the message unwittingly open the door to competitors, as the customers start wondering if they need to also see other options.

  In this step, you want to only detail the advances you've made that keep you competitive in the market. Keep your list short—don't inundate your customers with a lengthy list of features and benefits. Stick with the capabilities that are most closely aligned with your customers' original goals. And remember, in a Why

Stay conversation your competitive advances do not need to be differentiated. They don't need to be the best. They don't even need to be better. They just need to prove that you're advancing your solution *just like everyone else*, so there's really no reason to change. Your customers' original choice was correct, and it's keeping pace with their stated objectives.

NAVIGATING THE WHY PAY MORE CONVERSATION

As you read in Chapter 4, most organizations consider price increases "important" or "critical" to their growth—yet more than half are not confident in the way they message these increases. And since communicating a price increase falls to sales 60 percent of the time, having the skills to manage what most consider the most uncomfortable part of the conversation should be just as important as the increase itself.

Fortunately, you've already mastered most of this conversation with the Why Stay framework. The final step is to add the Why Pay More component by anchoring your customer on a higher price and then offering a loyalty discount.

Once you understand price anchoring, you'll notice it everywhere, for purchases large and small. A home seller might tell you, "The house down the street sold for 20 percent over asking price." Or when you see a $9, $7, and $6 glass of wine on a menu, the $9 glass serves as the anchor to make the $7 glass look more reasonable. It also leads you to think the $6 glass is inferior.

The odd thing about anchoring is that it works even when you know you are being anchored! Your brain can't help but take that mental shortcut when confronted with a decision involving uncertainty, so it's going to latch onto that reference point whether you want it to or not. And the mental shortcut is even simpler than you'd imagine. The brain anchors to the first number it hears—even if that number is utterly irrelevant to the topic at hand.

Sellers are often afraid of starting with an unreasonably high anchor—a place we've dubbed the "Bozo Zone" because it's so high it makes customers laugh—so sellers often set the initial price too low. That plays right into the hands of the customers. The distance between that unreasonably high price—where you would get laughed out of the room—and an unreasonably low price—where even your customers know no vendor would do business with them—is called the "Range of Reason."

In any price increase conversation, you want to start with the highest reasonable, credible offer within the Range of Reason. At first, it will feel too high. That's why *reasonable* and *credible* are so important. You're setting a high anchor that you can *reasonably* defend to your customer—even before that loyalty discount.

When you communicate a reasonably high target, you positively influence your customer's perception of renewing with you, and attaining the price increase you need. Research has shown there's a strong correlation between the first offer and the final price, and this effect holds true across cultures.

Here's an example of how this works in a Why Pay More conversation.

Assume you have an existing customer due for renewal and you need to introduce a minimum 2 percent price increase. When you introduce your price increase, there's a range of starting points you could use.

You could just ask for the 2 percent. But what do you think your customer's reaction would be? Your customer would want to negotiate, as a customer should, and you'd be lucky to end with the same price as you started.

So you use anchoring and your customer's Range of Reason to set a high target.

You have an additional challenge. You don't know the top end of your customer's Range of Reason. But you can be fairly sure your customer's top end is probably higher than you might be willing to try for. The top end might be 5 percent, but you might feel confident the customer would be willing to pay 3 percent.

You could ask for a 3 percent increase and be prepared to give a 1 percent discount, and neither you nor the customer will feel good about it. Again, though, you'd leave yourself little negotiating room to land at your desired target.

But if you set a high anchor with justification—competitive advances that will help your customer continue to meet his or her stated objectives—you can stretch your customer's Range of Reason to as high as 6 percent (Figure 12.2). Then provide a loyalty discount, which takes the price increase down to 4 percent.

Now you've obtained the price increase that's higher than your minimum and at the same time helped your customer feel better about getting a good discount.

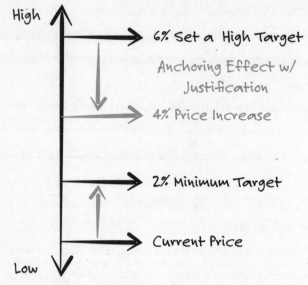

Figure 12.2 Setting a high anchor and combining it with a justified discount will get you more than your minimum price increase while still satisfying your customer.

And anchoring high doesn't always mean price alone. You could also anchor your customer on the length of the contract, the number of users, or anything else where you want to start higher than where you ultimately land.

NAVIGATING THE WHY EVOLVE CONVERSATION

While getting your customers to keep buying the same thing from you is important, retaining customers alone won't get you to your growth goals, even if customers happily accept your price increases. You need your customer to buy more from you—to purchase additional products or transition to higher-value solutions. In short, you need to evolve your relationship with your customers while still keeping the competition at bay.

The Why Evolve conversation is your opportunity to reset your customer's status quo on a higher plane. You're increasing customer share of wallet, deepening product penetration, enhancing contract value—you name it. And with each successful Why Evolve conversation, you're cementing the status quo, demonstrating results, and setting yourself up for further expansion conversations. Done right, there's continued value creation on both sides of the partnership.

But the Why Evolve conversation can also be tricky. You're asking customers to invest in a new solution—in other words, to make a change—when you're the incumbent. That means you have to balance your customers' need for change against your need to reinforce the status quo. They're already buying from you, and you want to keep it that way. So you want them to do something different . . . but only within the universe of your solutions. You need to show them that the cost of staying the same is too great to bear while at the same time keeping them from straying too far.

Your Why Evolve message is strongest when it reinforces the emotional elements of your customer relationship—the existing partnership and the collective progress you've made toward the customer's goals. The winning message from Chapter 7 spoke to the customer's head and heart. It communicated greater contrast, heightened the customer's sense of urgency, was found to be more convincing, and increased the likelihood the customer would purchase the new solution. Without this emotional foundation, you reduce the success of the rest of the conversation.

- **Step 1. Document Results.** You'll begin the Why Evolve conversation the same way you begin a Why Stay or Why Pay More conversation: by documenting the customer's results. Again, what you're looking to do here is to find a way to quantify the tenure and impact of your relationship. But then, instead of reinforcing the cost and risk of change, you're going to introduce the need to make a measured, considered evolution—with you as the trusted partner.

- **Step 2. Highlight evolving pressures.** The key to highlighting evolving pressures is combining those elements of the status quo that you want to reinforce with the seeds of change. Equally important, the evolving pressures you highlight need to feel logical, natural, and expected—things that inevitably occur in the course of doing business.

  You don't want to disrupt your customers at this stage, nor do you want to change their current thinking. You're acting as a good, honest partner, acknowledging the pressures they're starting to feel, that they likely want to address but haven't yet had the opportunity to. Such pressures might include things like new regulatory requirements, shifting consumer preferences, or industry trends.

  In this section, it's important to show pressures that have evolved from the ones they partnered with you to address instead of introducing radically new pressures they've never heard of or dealt with before.

If it is too revolutionary, you'll open the floodgates to the competition.

An effective way to introduce an evolving pressure is to set it up by introducing a piece of data or a perspective that highlights some tension between their status quo and their stated goals. For example, "There are some major demographic shifts happening in the consumer landscape. In fact, new research shows that just three groups of consumers will generate half of global urban consumer consumption growth from now through 2030." These shouldn't be the same insights you used in your acquisition conversations. What you want to do here is show how these external factors are changing and putting increased pressure on their business. And whatever you do, make sure these are pressures your new solution can help your customers solve! You don't want to raise a problem you don't have an answer for. That's a recipe for your customers to seek competing alternatives.

- **Step 3. Share "hard truths."** The "hard truths" form the "so what?" element of the evolving pressures you just shared. This is where you share what will happen as a consequence of the evolving pressures—why the customer should care. In this step, you're playing the role of a coach, a tough teacher, or a mentor who has the customer's best interest at heart but must tell the truth to make things better.

Emotional words are important. So you need to tell the hard truths, but do so using words and a tone that show you care and have a vested interest.

- **Step 4. Emphasize risk of no change.** The next step in the conversation is to link the cost and risk of not changing as the negative consequences of not heeding the hard truths. Be specific so the consequences of no action are clear. You're looking to touch multiple areas here—operational performance, business processes, financial performance—so you can tie into the aversion of the customers to Anticipated Regret and Blame. At the same time, don't be afraid to lean into the risks if the customers make a complete change to the competition. Ideally, you're going to be able to show that all the value you've built together over the course of the relationship could be torn away and they'd have to try to rebuild it from scratch with someone else.

Incidentally, if you're not having these types of candid conversations with your customers today, you need to start. You should be embedded and comfortable enough to be talking frankly with their teams—and for them to be sharing concerns honestly with you. This trust is the linchpin for the Why Evolve story, and it's the best way to frame risk in a way that benefits you, the incumbent. In fact, waiting too long to have these difficult conversations will give the competition an unnecessary opening. You'd hate for your customers to bring you a new perspective from the competition, asking why you hadn't addressed it given your privileged position as trusted partner.

- Step 5. Describe upside opportunity. The last step of the Why Evolve message framework is where you frame the new, future state you're envisioning. It's where you contrast the risk of no change with the upside opportunity of changing. Once again, you'll find value in the contrast.

  In this step, you're pivoting from risk to empowerment. One of the most powerful ways to do this is by using the you-phrasing language you read about in the last chapter to transfer ownership of the solution to your customer. In this case, ownership includes all the internal and external benefits resulting from making the change you're recommending. Instead of using a success story about another customer who made the change, you're making this customer the hero by painting a vision of them making the decision and successfully using the solution.

  Then close with what they need to do to get that value.

13

Expansion Messaging as a Commercial Strategy

I f your job is to lead teams, scale organizations, or design your company's commercial strategy, this chapter is for you.

Throughout this book, you've learned a series of useful frameworks that will help you make great tactical decisions to manage acute commercial moments with existing customers. But when you're trying to drive companywide transformation, you also need to know the obstacles you're likely to face. These obstacles are anchored in your old customer engagement motion. To get the full value from everything you've learned in this book, you must break this motion.

In this chapter, you'll learn the three key moves that support this strategic transformation:

- Changing your messaging cadence in the customer life cycle

- Changing the content of your business reviews

- Changing the focus of your launch meetings

But first, let's take a look at what so many organizations get wrong.

If you're like most organizations, your customer engagement motion follows a logical flow. First, you sign a new client. Then, your salesperson hands the client off to a post-sales team, such as a customer success manager, or maybe someone with a different title but the same basic function. Then, that customer success manager works with the customer on adoption, utilization, reporting, and fixing any problems that crop up.

During this time, your salesperson is only peripherally involved with the account. They might be doing check-ins with the customer, but the salesperson is mostly staying out of the way as the solution gets implemented. It's only when the contract nears its end that the salesperson re-engages, because the salesperson knows this is when the customer has to make a decision. Do they renew and extend the contract? Do they expand into new offerings from your company? Do they move to a competitor? Do they figure out a way to do this as an in-house solution?

Now, assuming you've taught your sales team the Why Stay and Why Evolve frameworks you've learned about in this book, where will the sales team apply them? Most likely in the same place where they normally re-engage with the customer: the end of the contract (Figure 13.1).

Figure 13.1 Most sellers wait until a contract is about to expire before re-engaging.

This is a mistake.

Before explaining why, let's take a look at some of the beliefs that drive your salespeople's engagement strategy.

There are two possible reasons salespeople don't engage the customer until the end of a sales cycle:

1. **The salesperson might have sold the customer everything there was to buy.** As a result, the salesperson is focused on finding new customers who can make a purchase now. There's some legitimacy to this approach, though most salespeople would be better served by staying engaged with the customer over the length of the contract. Remember, one of your advantages with existing customers is their Status Quo Bias. Reinforcing the customer's relationship with their salesperson over the length of the contract gives you one more piece of status quo, in this case the seller-customer relationship, to leverage in your favor when it comes time for a renewal or contract extension.

2. **The salesperson believes that customers don't want to be sold something new while they're already under contract.** It feels "wrong" or "rude" to present an existing customer with upgrades or additional services they should consider buying when the contract isn't yet at its end. Instead, it seems best to let the customer get to the end of the contract before trying to sell them something more. Plus, the customer is likely to have experienced more "value" toward the end of the contract, which should make it easier to then sell them the next thing. At least, that's the rationalization.

The underlying flaw in both these mindsets becomes apparent when you look at what this means to the customer experience. When you take this approach, your customer is experiencing a Messaging Void from your organization over most of the length of the contract (Figure 13.2).

Figure 13.2 When sellers don't engage with customers throughout the contract life, they create a Messaging Void.

At first glance, you might think, "That's okay. Our customer is safely under contract with us. We can wait until the end to message to them." But that's an incorrect—and dangerous—assumption.

Is it really true that your customer is not experiencing any messaging during the Messaging Void you've created in your engagement strategy? Of course not.

Your customer is being bombarded with messaging—from your competitors, your partners, and industry analysts, just to name a few (Figure 13.3).

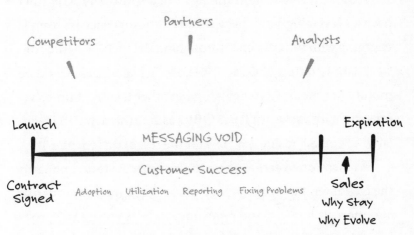

Figure 13.3 In the absence of your messaging, competitors fill the void.

And what kind of message are they bringing to your customer? The most disruptive messages they can come up with.

Your competition knows you're the status quo, and their first goal is to disrupt that status quo. So, while you've created this Messaging Void out of a mistaken assumption that your customers will be grateful, you're also allowing your competition to reset your customer's beliefs around how they should solve their core business problems.

When you allow your Messaging Void to be filled by others who are not your friends and who are, in fact, actively working against your interests, by the time your sales team delivers your message at the end of the contract, it's too late. You've already failed to articulate value. In fact, your customers already know a lot of what you want to talk to them about because they've heard it from everyone else, and their first question for you is, *"Why haven't you been talking to us about any of this?"*

Now you might be thinking, "That's not true. We don't have a Messaging Void, because our customer success team is engaging with the customer throughout the lifetime of the contract with Quarterly Business Reviews." (*Note:* These could be monthly or biannual reviews, or any other length of time, but for simplicity's sake, we'll use QBRs as shorthand for any regularly scheduled business review for the rest of this chapter.)

As mentioned earlier, the customer success team onboards the customer during the launch phase. They track metrics like adoption, utilization, and reporting, and if there are any problems, they fix them along the way (hopefully, applying the Why Forgive framework if necessary). And they communicate these things to the customer during QBRs (Figure 13.4). Isn't that filling the Messaging Void?

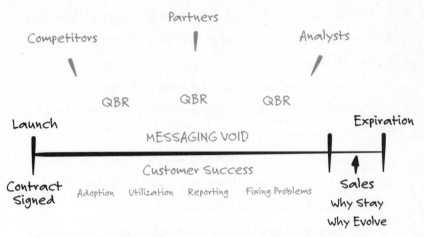

Figure 13.4 Activity does not equal messaging.

Certainly, there's a lot of activity taking place during this period, and there are, presumably, a lot of conversations happening. But what's likely *not* happening is any sort of messaging that communicates value. In reality, most of these conversations are more accurately described as data exchanges and status updates. And it's often at a level that is non-strategic, which is also why the first QBR an executive attends is often the last QBR that executive attends. Why? Because you're not speaking to her issues and concerns.

Since messaging is properly understood as the communication of value, these QBR conversations don't fill the Messaging Void.

And here is where the Why Stay and Why Evolve frameworks come to the rescue. Those frameworks were explicitly built to communicate value, and, as it turns out, they're also great frameworks for QBRs.

In your early QBRs, you should be telling your Why Stay story, which is a story of why the customer made a good choice. It shows the customer that everything is going according to plan and reinforces the decision they made to choose you.

But before too long, you need to shift your QBRs to tell a Why Evolve story.

This isn't something you want to save for the end of the contract. In fact, what our research shows is that if you save it for the very end, you'll disrupt their thinking.

If you disrupt their thinking too much, you're essentially pushing them to look at what other options might be out there that they haven't yet explored. You don't want to take that risk at the end of the contract. Instead, you want to introduce the idea of evolving when you're still in the comfortable confines of the contract. Your communication cadence should look more like Figure 13.5.

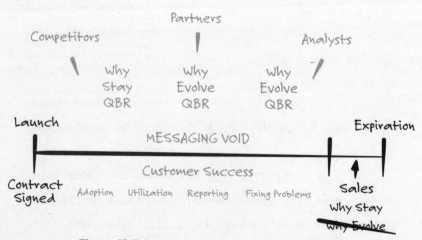

Figure 13.5 Introduce your Why Evolve message when you're safe within the contract.

When you change your messaging cadence and use the frameworks as the flow of your QBRs, you're actually helping customer success do the most important job that customer success has, which is communicating value.

Nevertheless, you should be prepared for some resistance from your customer success team.

Many customer success managers are reluctant to do anything that feels like "selling" to their customers. They want their customers to believe the customer success manager is grateful for their business and is working incessantly to delight them every day. In fact, they likely pride themselves on their "niceness." They'll even go so far as to describe themselves as the people the customer can trust (as opposed to salespeople).

The last thing a customer success manager wants to do is upset this view of themselves by doing something that feels like selling. And to be clear, we aren't suggesting that you turn your customer success people into salespeople. But what they do need to become is *value communicators*.

Pleasing the customer is undoubtedly an important part of their job. But your company didn't invest in these support teams *only* to make sure a customer is happy. Your company invested in these teams to make sure a customer is *retained*, and ultimately, to make sure your business with the customer expands.

And if that's the goal, how do you make it happen?

You do that by articulating value.

And that leads to the third change you need to make to your commercial strategy.

To understand the next change, you need to quickly review the content in the Why Stay and Why Evolve frameworks. These message frameworks are markedly different from one another. Each has five motions, five message components, that build the story. But one focuses on reinforcing Status Quo Bias, while the other introduces a little disruption.

However, there's one component that's the same for both, and that is the first step: Documenting Results (Figure 13.6).

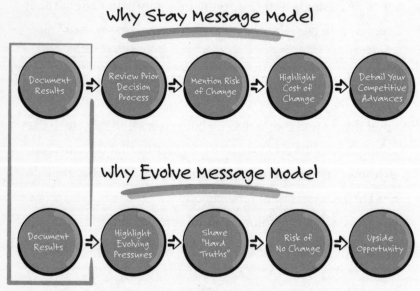

Figure 13.6 Documenting Results is the common element.

Interestingly, what we've seen in customer after customer who have rolled out these frameworks is that this is often the weakest, and most difficult, part of the message to master. And yet, this is the component that will make the most difference when it comes to filling your Messaging Void, starting with the launch.

MASTER THE LAUNCH

Picture the typical launch meeting. If you sell a relatively high-ticket item, it probably takes place at the customer's headquarters, in the "good" conference room, with all the team members from both sides arrayed around a big mahogany table. For smaller customers or lower ticket items, it might take place virtually. Either way, there are introductions and a round of congratulations for finally getting the project off the ground. Then the customer success lead asks the customer what their goals for the implementation are.

And that's where things begin to go wrong.

When you ask the customer what their implementation goals are, you'll often elicit a response like, "We're looking to roll out to X many people within this time frame, integrate it with these internal systems, and complete everything by X date."

If you're the customer success lead, you say, "Great!" You diligently write these things down. These become your goals, and thus become the goals you report back on in your QBRs.

Now imagine you've been fortunate enough to get the most senior executive sponsor in the room for this all-important launch meeting. Did she buy your solution because she desperately wanted to track how many people are using it, how much time they've spent in it, and when the integrations happen? Of course not.

She bought it to enable larger, more strategic business goals, and because you skipped over them to focus on tactical milestones, this will probably be the last meeting she attends.

That's a missed messaging opportunity.

The launch meeting should set the agenda for all subsequent meetings and serve as the foundation of your expansion strategy.

Don't rush through the discussion of success metrics. Linger in it. And don't settle for the easily collectable but often unimportant metrics. Use the Triple Metric you learned about in Chapter 11 to guide the conversation to get to the important metrics—the ones that matter at the executive levels. Resist the urge to simply jot down the customer's initial implementation goals and instead push for the customer to describe the Project level, Business Unit level, and Corporate level goals they want to achieve with this initiative.

And don't be afraid to ask tough questions, such as how they're going to measure those goals.

Measuring these goals shouldn't fall only on customer success. Often, the most important goals will only be measurable by metrics available on the customer side. That's okay.

What you need is agreement that those are the goals by which success will be measured. And that both sides owe it to each other to track performance against those goals and report back to the team. If you're used to being responsible for all reporting on project performance, this might feel strange to you. But what you'll see is that these are the goals that motivate executive engagement.

Also, be prepared for some customer resistance here. Lower level people in the meeting will want to pick the easy goals that are entirely your responsibility as a vendor. You can easily measure usage for them, as an example. But if you let those be the only metrics captured, you've now guaranteed that your executive sponsor will lose faith in your ability to impact their organization. Those metrics aren't meaningful to her.

And the ripple effect of the failure to capture meaningful goals is profound. Remember how your Why Stay story and your Why Evolve story start? By Documenting Results. If you don't do a good job capturing the real goals during your launch meeting, you'll have nothing meaningful to tie your messaging back to during key messaging moments in the customer relationship. By the time you get to the end of the contract, you'll be left with nothing much more than, "Stick with us. We've been nice."

FILL THE VOID

To take full advantage of what you've learned in this book, you need to break your old engagement motion and redesign your commercial strategy. Don't let old habits get in the way of executing on these frameworks. Lead your team to a new level of performance by:

- Changing your messaging cadence across the customer life cycle

- Changing the content and flow of your business reviews

- Changing the focus of your launch meetings

When you do that, you'll fill your Messaging Void with conversations that communicate value from the beginning to the end of the contract. And your new commercial strategy will naturally reinforce your customer's Status Quo Bias so much that it will create a nearly impenetrable psychological shield—protecting your relationship with your customer from your competitors (Figure 13.7).

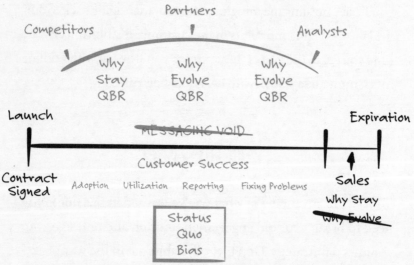

Figure 13.7 Keep and grow customer relationships through value-based conversations.

Ultimately, applying this new messaging motion means you can fully leverage the frameworks you've learned to keep and grow your customers.

≥ 14 ≤

Parting Thoughts

Over the course of this book, you've learned the frameworks, situational fluency, and tactical skills your organization needs to message effectively to existing customers in the four acute commercial moments—renewals, price increases, upsells, and apologies.

And yet underneath it all, there's a broader story to tell. It's the story of the difference between assertions made from "best-practices" capture and assertions made through applying scientific rigor to your understanding how your customers frame value and make choices.

Much of what passes for thought leadership in sales and marketing is really best-practices capture. People at companies are surveyed. They're asked how they do things. And then an analyst summarizes those findings and says, in essence, "Do what these people do, because they are in the top quartile of performance with respect to their peers."

There are challenges with that type of analysis.

The most important challenge is that the assumption of cause and effect is unfounded. Just because people engaging in one set of behaviors happen to be clustered near the top of their peers doesn't mean the behaviors themselves caused the performance. It could be any one of hundreds of other factors that caused the performance. For example, it could be that the most successful companies happen to be in a market space that's very hot, and because companies tend to copy each other's behavior, they all are using the same tactics.

Does that mean the tactics caused the performance? No. Any tactics would have worked in that situation.

The fact that those companies chose to copy each other tells us nothing insightful. It simply captures herd behavior.

Might it still work? It might. But because you're simply copying tactics without an underlying understanding of how or why they work, you're going to find yourself in a position where you have to guess how you should implement those tactics. You might be successful at the end, but you're going to have to work really hard to get there.

Throughout this book you've seen a different approach. You haven't been reading about best-practices capture. Instead, you've learned the results of many studies conducted across thousands of participants around the world.

These studies were funded by us, but they were designed and conducted by independent scientists. These scientists designed these studies purposefully, so you could see true cause and effect, something that can't be seen through best-practices capture.

The net effect is that not only can you apply these messaging techniques in the described situations, but you also can be situationally fluent in unique situations, because you have an understanding of how your customer frames value and makes choices.

A useful way of thinking about this is that best-practices capture is analogous to our understanding of the solar system before Copernicus. When scientists believed that everything revolved around the earth, it made it difficult to track the movement of the other planets, but not impossible. You simply kept gathering observational data and trying to come up with very complex mathematical models to explain the observed behavior of the planets.

But once Copernicus reoriented thinking to the idea that the planets revolved around the sun, everything got easier. You understood why your observational data looked like it did, and now the math got easier, as well. And that led to much more accurate predictions for where the planets would be in the sky.

The same pre-Copernicus problem exists if you try to understand marketing and sales through the lens of following best practices. You can observe customer behavior, but it is very difficult to predict that behavior. You have to come up with increasingly complex models to match your observational data with your results.

But when you move from a best-practices imitation approach and instead view your customer's decision making through the lens of Status Quo Bias, your ability to predict customer behavior in unique situations grows.

Just as Copernicus swapped out the earth for the sun in the center of his maps, sales and marketing professionals need to swap out best-practices capture for an understanding of Status Quo Bias as the center of their maps.

When you combine that knowledge with an understanding of concepts like the power of anchoring, emotional decision making, and visual storytelling, you'll have a framework to create the most impactful messages, regardless of the uniqueness of your situation.

Use these tools often. Use them well. And thank you for the gift of your time and attention.

Erik Peterson
Chief Executive Officer
Corporate Visions, Inc.

⇒ Appendix ⇐

Real-World Examples

N ow that you've learned the theory, studied the frameworks, and mastered the skills you need to deliver your expansion message, you're probably wondering how these elements all come together in a real-world scenario. "Hmph!" we hear you grumble. "Might be nice to see what all this stuff looks like in the light of day."

Happy to oblige!

In the pages that follow, you'll see examples of two complete stories—messages developed within the applicable frameworks, together with supporting visuals, designed to be delivered in live meetings with existing customers.*

The first comes from our own archive (yes, we subscribe wholeheartedly to the "put your money where your mouth is" theory of business). The second is a message developed in partnership with a client for its sellers to deliver to their own customers.

---

* To protect our clients' privacy, we've removed identifying details and renamed each company "Acme Corporation."

CORPORATE VISIONS WHY STAY (RENEWAL) MESSAGE FOR ACME CORPORATION

When Acme Corp., one of our longtime clients, was nearing the end of its contract term, we decided the best way to convince the company that our new (at the time) Why Stay message framework was valid was to use it to develop and deliver the renewal message.

And in case you're wondering, the client did, in fact, renew the contract.

Here's the story that won the renewal, and the corresponding simple, concrete visual to support that story. Review the story and the visual—then use the Why Stay planner to practice your own renewal message.

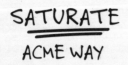

Three years ago, you were focused on improving sales rep productivity. Whether that's deal size or velocity or win rates, the research showed that you could get the most traction toward that goal by improving the customer conversation.

But that research was essentially *descriptive*. You also needed the "how"—tactical ways to apply the theory to the Acme Corp. way of selling. How do you differentiate your solutions? How do you elevate sales conversations to the executive level? And how do you saturate the field in this approach?

You turned to us because only with Corporate Visions can you tie the research to specific real-world applications in marketing, selling, and learning. And it's been working.

In fact, these numbers—600, 80, and 8—tell a story about your progress.

- In a third-party study, 600 of your reps reported on one deal.

- From that sample alone, $80 million in revenue was directly influenced by the new model that you've put into place.

- Just last quarter, you saw 8 percent year-over-year revenue growth.

Now you know how difficult it is for Sales Ops to prove that those results are tied directly to the new messaging and skills you're rolling out. But you've also been hearing stories from the field about their successes.

- One sales leader said that by being more intentional and deliberate about applying these conversation skills, last year was his team's best year ever.

- A seller in another division said that role-playing executive feedback helped him close a deal just days later.

- And another said that these conversations created, quote, "such awe" that the prospect immediately signed the deal.

It's all driven by the street-level skills that you've developed with Corporate Visions.

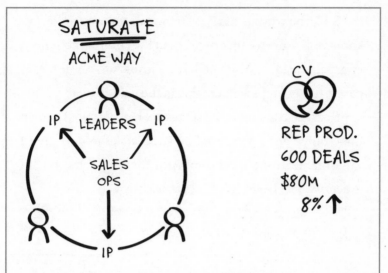

But it hasn't been easy to get to this point. You debated with multiple stakeholders, getting consensus over nearly five months of meetings. Then you worked even harder to weave Corporate Visions' work into the Acme Corp way of selling.

- You chose to align our IP with each step of your process.

- You created unlimited access to it in all the tools your reps use every day.

- You embedded the training into your onboarding.

All that paid off, because now you've truly saturated all your sellers in the same IP. That's what creates the level of change that makes a difference in your performance.

Still, the truth is that you're not all the way there. We know you've been concerned about the commitment from your sales leaders. You need those leaders to reinforce, to coach, to hold reps accountable in the field.

Because right now, the stakes are high. It's well known that you've been pressured by vocal stakeholders about the organization's direction. And there's been a recent executive-level mandate to stay the course.

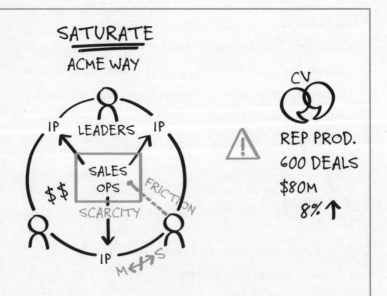

When you think about it, stepping away from your current approach means dialing back this saturation. It means putting a hurdle in between your sellers and the messages and skills you want them to use—those that have already demonstrated the ability to win.

Think of this as a scarcity model. When you limit access to the IP, the signal loses some of its impact. It degrades when it has to travel farther.

- That's partly because there's friction involved. Say you've got a big client meeting in a month, and it would be a great time to give your team some training. But you have to get a PO. You have to limit how many sellers can attend so that it fits in your budget. Maybe you figure it might be easier to do something else instead—or nothing at all.

- You also break that alignment between marketing and sales. Without full access, the IP won't be embedded in your systems such as Salesforce. You lose the built-in reporting and tracking in your LMS. You're no longer putting your messages in context.

- Plus, you worked with us as a collaboration partner to innovate this model. The scarcity approach *feels* more frugal, but you'd actually be paying significantly more money per engagement without it. That's especially true when you consider that your certified facilitators would no longer be licensed to deliver training.

When you make the IP scarce, your productivity will by definition take a slide. As you know, with the pressure you're facing, you simply can't afford that right now.

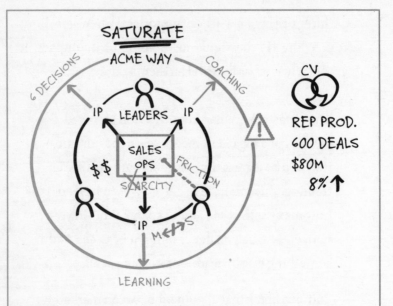

Although your sellers have learned a lot in the past three years, that doesn't mean it's time to retreat to a scarcity model. Instead, you need to drive this saturation even further into the field. The good news is that this requires virtually no change on your part. All you have to do is stick with what you've had budgeted all these years.

When you do, you'll have new ways to influence rep productivity:

- First, you'll help your enablement team create even more powerful conversations around the key decisions buyers make during their relationship with you. We've done new research with surprising results that informs our continued IP development.

- Second, you'll help your sales leaders model and coach the IP. Leaders excel when they can see written feedback of how their people were coached after exhibiting their skills. So you'll make coaching more prescriptive and consistent by showing your managers feedback from our experts, and then showing them how to follow the same rubric in their own coaching.

- And third, you'll have more opportunities to tie in inline, virtual microlearning. You've used us to deliver many events virtually. Now you'll take the next step to make virtual training even more effective by distilling content to the most granular level, delivering it repeatedly with skills practice, and embedding it into the systems your reps already use.

Why Stay Planner

Target Contact and Customer:

Document Results
The business change your solution created and how the results were measured

Prior Decisions
Describe the prior decision process and the key decision-makers involved

Risk of Change
Mention risks to the business as well as personal risks of making a change

Cost of Change
Highlight the direct and or indirect costs of change

Competitive Advances
Describe the solution improvements introduced since the original decision

Price Increase (if applicable)
Anchor high with the new price before giving a timed loyalty discount

FINANCIAL SERVICES WHY EVOLVE MESSAGE

Another client, a firm that provides technology solutions and processing services to large banks, turned to us for help transitioning existing customers away from its on-premise software products to a full outsourcing arrangement. This message was tricky, because the client was also the provider of the on-premise software! And even though the new arrangement would be much more profitable for our client, its sellers were nervous about starting that conversation. This story supported the sellers' situational fluency by giving them the framework of the message but also the space and coaching to insert client-specific detail and "reaction" questions to truly personalize the interaction.

Here's the story they developed, and the corresponding visual.

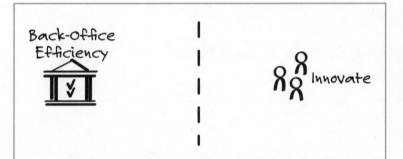

The entire financial services industry has been intensely focused on increasing efficiency to manage costs and relieve margin pressure. And working with us, you've made tremendous progress toward making your back office more efficient.

[Presenter: Replace the following ideas with customer-specific successes, ideally with quantifiable proof, such as efficiency gains, productivity improvements, or cost reductions.]

- You've worked with us to automate critical processes and workflows such as core processing and item processing.

- Now it's easier and faster to run your bank and comply with evolving regulations.

Yet despite these gains, many of your peers are questioning whether processing speed and back-office efficiency are enough to remain as lean as you need to be . . . and keep and grow your customer base. They're beginning to recognize that innovation beyond the back office is the only path forward.

[Presenter: Ask a reaction question, such as "How has your back office changed in the last XX years since you started working with us?"]

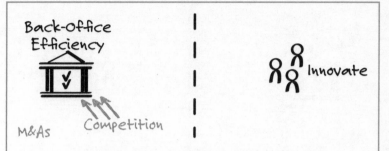

That's because pressure on both these fronts for banks like yours has amped up. For one thing, mergers and acquisitions are becoming the norm. And if you're adding new banks every year or 18 months, that rapid growth can strain your technology infrastructure. It's a scramble to get everyone on the same systems and ramp up your capacity—not to mention keep everything secure and compliant.

Meanwhile, your competition is changing. When you first started working with us, you were worried about other financial institutions competing on roughly the same criteria. And you've done a good job holding them at bay.

But now you also need to fend off new players—technology start-ups that didn't even originate in financial services but have flexible new technology that customers love. Meanwhile, savvy financial institutions that were once traditional competitors are catching onto this and launching their own products and services to take on the fintechs. So now you're getting squeezed from all three directions.

[*Presenter: Ask a reaction question, such as "What changes are you seeing from a competitive perspective? How have your bank's M&A activities affected your infrastructure and capacity?"*]

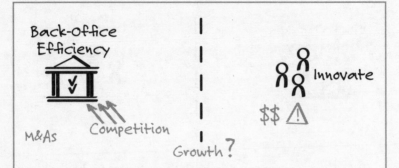

But while innovation is the answer, it's tough to implement new ideas given all the effort and expense it takes just to support your key processing systems.

Plus, innovation is fraught in financial services. Banks have to navigate layer upon layer of regulations and compliance concerns that ordinary companies don't. Most banks are torn between being open enough to give your customers a good experience, yet controlled enough that you don't risk breaches or damage to your margin or reputation.

Containing these risks pits you against your shareholders' and business owners' expectations for top-line growth. If growth is hindered or stalls, it won't matter how efficient your core and item processing have become. Not only will you fail to produce the gains you sought, but your ability to deliver what customers need could lag far enough behind competitors that you risk losing relevance and market share.

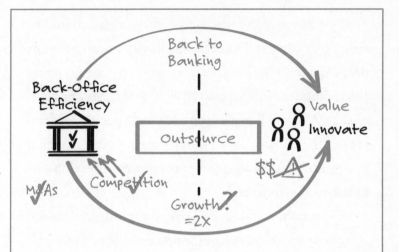

These dynamics are causing banks like yours to rethink their strategy. All the work you've done around back-office efficiency is more necessary than ever ... but so is running your business in a way that continually brings new value to customers.

You've been able to do both until now because you've been using our in-house solutions to keep things manageable in the back office. But the changing market and competition and customer demands are now hitting at such a pace that splitting your focus will start holding you back. The key is to refocus all your resources on their original mission: the business of banking. That means figuring out what customers need next from a financial and banking perspective—while keeping things running behind the scenes.

And that's why many of our long-time in-house clients are migrating to our new outsourcing center.

By outsourcing your resource-intensive functions like core processing and item processing, you can get your people back to banking. You'll stay on top of emerging risks without devoting yourself 24/7 to security and compliance. And you'll bypass the back-end operational complexity that slows down innovation. In doing so, you'll open yourself up to big new opportunities to develop customer-focused offerings.

Ultimately, you'll address risk, complexity, and speed all at once when you outsource processing functions with strategic growth in mind. In fact, according to our "Annual Outsourcing Report," banks that have transformed their businesses in this way are experiencing twice as much growth as their peers.

And that's what you're going to hear about next . . .

Why Evolve Planner

Target Contact and Customer:

Document Results
Quantify the tenure and impact of your partnership, and the results achieved to date

Evolving Pressures
Describe pressures as a natural progression, not a surprise or disruption

Hard Truths
Share missed opportunities that are hindering their performance

Risk of No Change
Underscore the potential risks of not evolving or keeping up

Upside Opportunity
Use "you" language to transfer the benefits of making a change to your customer

CORPORATE VISIONS

Index

Page numbers followed by *f* indicate figures.

A

accountability, ownership and, 30, 31
acquisition
    conversations, 17*f*
    customer, 7*f*, 20, 29, 30, 33*f*
    expansion messaging and, 32–33,
        33*f*
    with status quo bias, disrupt or
        defend, 6–16
    with status quo bias, not
        disrupting, 21–24
    with status quo bias defeated,
        16–21
activity, messaging unequal to, 183*f*
add-on sale, 29*f*, 70*f*
anchor
    of price increase with discount
        justified, 67
    of price increase with timed
        discount, 55
    pricing, 58–61
anchoring effect
    loyalty discount and, 167, 170*f*
    price increase conversations with,
        60–61
    range of reason and, 168–169
Anderson, Christopher J., 7–8

"Annual Outsourcing Report," 208
anticipated regret and blame
    with before and after proof, 19
    reinforced, 43
    status quo bias and, 8, 10–11
    with status quo bias reinforced,
        23–24
apology. *See also* Why Forgive
    B2B organization and, 97, 102
    components, 95–96
    confidence in effectiveness of, 93*f*
    Corporate Visions survey and,
        91–92
    formal process for, 93*f*
    framework, 96–97
    importance of, 91–93, 92*f*
    incumbent advantage and, 89
    as must-win commercial moment,
        xx, 3
    with problem explained, 96
    with regret, 8, 10–11, 23–24, 43,
        96, 112–113
    with repair offer, 96, 111–112
    with repentance, declaration of,
        96, 112
    with responsibility,
        acknowledgment of, 96, 112

apology (*continued*)
 revenue with, 91–92
 science, 89–97
 situational fluency and, 132–134
 "sorry" and, 113–114, 132, 133
 SRP and, 90*f*, 94–95, 104, 114
 as working tool, 114–115

B

B2B organization
 apology, 97, 102
 on price increase, 47, 51
 with retention, underinvesting
   in, 29
 service failure scenario and, 104
 SRP and, 94–95
 Why Change and, 20
Bain & Company, 48
best-practices capture, 191–193
Bozo Zone, 168
brain
 decision-making part of, 10, 18,
   173
 risk aversion, subconscious
   thinking and, 11
 thinking and, 11, 148
brain science, 3, 12
business unit level, expansion seller
   and, 137

C

Campbell, Joseph, 156
change. *See also* perceived cost of
   change; risk of change; Why
   Change
 contrast required for, 18
 inciting, 73
 risk of no, 84–85, 174–175
 selection difficulty and, 10
 Why Evolve and, 149

Cialdini, Robert, 61
close (incident) rate, 20
compensation, SRP and, 95
competitive advances
 unconsidered need and, 45
 in Why Pay More conversation,
   66–67
 Why Stay conversation and,
   166–167
 in Why Stay message, 44–45
competitive differentiation, 32
competitors, filling void in absence
   of messaging, 181*f*
confidence
 in apology effectiveness, 93*f*
 price increase conversations with,
   57
 price increase with, 48–50, 49*f*, 50*f*
 problem resolution and customer,
   108*f*
context effect
 defined, xviii*f*
 environmental factors and,
   xviii–xix, 7*f*
 example, xvii
contract
 messaging void with, 180*f*
 salesperson believing customer
   unwilling to buy new while
   under, 180
 with sellers re-engaging before
   expiration, 179*f*
 Why Evolve message introduced
   within, 184*f*
contrast
 change with required, 18
 for customers, 148–149
 customers stories with, 142–145
 status quo bias defeated with,
   18–19

conversation, 5. *See also* Why
Evolve conversation; Why Pay
More conversation; Why Stay
conversation
"acquisition," 17*f*
customer relationship and
value-based, 190*f*
"expansion," 6, 22*f*
price increase, 57–68, 62*f*–63*f*, 65*f*
*Conversations That Win the Complex
Sale* (Peterson and Riesterer),
5, 122
conversion rate, 71*f*
Copernicus, 193
corporate level, expansion seller and,
137
Corporate Visions, Why Stay
message, 196–203
Corporate Visions survey
apology and, 91–92
on customer acquisition, 29
executive emotions and, 114
interactive visual and, 153
renewal and, 29*f*, 31*f*, 33*f*
upsell and, 70
visual storytelling and, 150–151
"you-phrasing" and, 157
cost. *See also* price increase
of change with Why Pay More
conversation, 66
of change with Why Stay
conversation, 164, 166
perceived cost of change, 7, 9–10,
18, 23, 43–44
price increase conversation with
external, 60
"sunk," 27–28, 27*f*
credibility
expansion sale and, 152*f*
perceptions lifted, 39

suppliers with apology and,
109*f*–111*f*
cross-selling, 130
customer
confidence with problem
resolution, 108*f*
contrast for, 148–149
with current solution and status
quo bias reinforced, 86*f*
discount for, 25
expansion, 3, 7*f*
messaging void and, 180*f*
painting picture for, 147–148
picture superiority effect and,
146–147
price increase and view of, 49*f*
retention, 91, 131–132, 145
simplicity with infographics for,
148
stories with contrast, 142–145
in "sweet spot," 26
thinking of, 148
unwilling to buy new while under
contract, 180
value-based conversations and
relationships with, 190*f*
"we-phrasing" for, 157
Why Evolve conversation with
success of, 72
"you-phrasing" with, 155–159,
175
customer acquisition, 20
Corporate Visions survey on, 29
customer expansion not equal
to, 7*f*
renewal message and, 30, 33*f*

D

decision process
in Why Pay More conversation, 66

decision process (*continued*)
  in Why Stay conversation,
    161–162
  in Why Stay message, 42
decision-making, brain and, 10, 18,
    173
Decision Science, 5, 6, 21, 113
demand generation, 29–30, 33
discount
  for customer, 25
  high anchor with loyalty, 170*f*
  justified in Why Pay More
    conversation, 67
  loyalty, 59, 65, 167, 170*f*
  price increase conversations with
    time-sensitive, 59
  price increase to anchor timed, 55

E

emotion
  executive, 13–15, 114
  relationship reinforcement and,
    76, 77*f*, 78*f*–80*f*, 82–87, 82*f*,
    86*f*
  service failure scenario with
    negative, 100–101
emotionless executive, myth of
  in gain frame, 13*f*
  in loss frame, 14*f*, 15*f*
  with persuadability in loss frame,
    15*f*
  status quo bias with, 11–16
employees, 111, 113
  engagement, 137
  health and wellness program for,
    58, 67
  HR benefits for, 100
  layoffs in workplace, 12–16
  retention rates, 36, 41, 58, 65, 67
  retirement plan for, 36–37, 41, 44

satisfaction scores, 41, 65
  turnover, 84
environmental factor, Context Effect
    and, xviii–xix, 7*f*
evolve. *See* Why Evolve
executive, myth of emotionless,
    11–16, 13*f*, 14*f*, 15*f*
executive emotion
  Corporate Vision's survey and,
    114
  study, 13–15
"expansion" conversation
  Decision Science and, 6
  status quo bias reinforced with, 22*f*
expansion customer, 3, 7*f*
expansion messaging
  acquisition and, 32–33, 33*f*
  mission of, 25–26
  no clear ownership of renewal
    message with, 30–32, 31*f*
  power of incumbency and, 26–29,
    26*f*, 27*f*, 28*f*
  underinvest in retention with,
    29–30, 29*f*
expansion messaging, as commercial
    strategy
  with activity not equal to
    messaging, 183*f*
  explanation of, 177–186
  with launch, mastering of,
    187–189
  messaging void and, 180*f*
  with results documented, 186*f*
  with salesperson believing
    customers not buying new
    items while under contract,
    180
  with salesperson selling all
    available items to customer,
    179

with sellers waiting for contract
expiration before re-engaging,
179f
with void filled, 189–190, 190f
with void filled by competitors,
181f
with Why Evolve message
introduced within contract,
184f
expansion sale
apology science and, 89–97
with credibility and memorability,
152f
ownership versus partnership in,
155–158
visual storytelling for, 145–155
expansion seller
believing customers not buying
new items while under
contract, 180
corporate, business unit and
project levels with, 137
customer sold all available items
by, 179
customer stories with contrast
and, 142–145
importance of, 135–136
number plays and, 140–142
with results documented, 136–145
Triple Metric and, 137–139,
138f
expansion seller, advanced skills for
Why Evolve conversation and,
170–175
Why Pay More conversation and,
167–170, 170f
Why Stay conversation and,
160–167, 165f
"An Exploration of the Structure of
Effective Apologies," 96

F

financial services, Why Evolve
message framework, 205–209
forgive. See Why Forgive
formal apology process, 93f
401k, 36–37, 41, 44

G

gain frame
moving toward, 165f
myth of emotionless executive in, 13f
prospect theory and, 18, 84, 165
Geoffrion, Cheryl, 5
growth, revenue, 82, 122, 137, 197

H

hand-drawn image, 151
hard truths, 83–84, 173–174
health and wellness program, for
employees, 58, 67
herd behavior, 192
hero
mentor and journey of, 156
product as, 75–76, 81, 126
"vendor-as-hero" language, 157
The Hero with a Thousand Faces
(Campbell), 156
human resources (HR) benefits, for
employees, 100

I

imagination, self-relevance and
invoking, 156
incident (close) rate, 20
incumbency, power of
customers receive initial value after
signing deal, 26f
expansion messaging and, 26–29
"sunk cost" mentality and, 27f
as "sure bet," 28f

incumbent advantage
    anticipated regret and blame with,
      43
    apology and, 89
    failure to exploit, 28–29
    losing, 131
    picture superiority effect and, 147
    with pressures highlighted, 83
    renewal message and, 31f, 32
    "sunk cost" and, 27–28, 27f
    undermined, 68, 72
    Why Evolve message framework
      and, 87, 129
    "Why Stay Renewal Study" and,
      35–37
infographics, simplicity with, 148
initiation, SRP and, 94
InsideSales.com, 152
insight, price increase and, 55
intellectual property (IP), 199–202
interactive visual, 153
International Journal of Sales
    Transformation, 153
IP (intellectual property), 199–202
iPhone, 129
item processing, 205, 207, 208

J

Journal of Business & Industrial
    Marketing, 94

K

Kahneman, Daniel, 18, 84, 165–166

L

language
    decision-making part of brain
      with, 173
    "vendor-as-hero," 157
    "you-phrasing," 155–159, 175

launch, mastering, 187–189
layoff, in workplace, 12–16
Lee, Nick, 6, 57, 64, 75, 99, 153
Listen, Watch, and Take Notes,
    154–155
loss frame
    moving away from, 165f
    myth of emotionless executive in,
      14f, 15f
    prospect theory and, 18, 84
loyalty discount, 59, 65, 167, 170f

M

marketer, as mentor, 156–157
memorability, expansion sale and,
    152f
mentor
    with hard truths, 173
    hero guided by, 156
    seller and marketer as, 156–157
messaging. *See also* expansion
    messaging; Why Evolve
    message framework; Why Stay
    message
    activity unequal to, 183f
    competitors filling void in absence
      of, 181f
    renewal, 30–32, 31f, 33f, 40, 52,
      63f, 64
    retention, 23–24, 65
    void, 180–184, 180f, 186, 190
microlearning, 203
must-win commercial moments,
    xx–xxi, 3. *See also* apology; price
    increase; renewal; upsell

N

no clear ownership
    with expansion messaging, 31f
    of renewal message, 30–32, 31f

number play
  example of, 141
  expansion seller and, 140–142

O

opportunity
  upside, 175
  Why Evolve and, 150
outsourcing, 205, 208
ownership
  accountability and, 30, 31
  expansion messaging with no
    clear, 31f
  expansion sale with partnership
    versus, 155–158
  renewal message with no clear,
    30–32, 31f

P

partnership versus ownership, in
    expansion sale, 155–158
pay more. See Why Pay More
    conversation
perceived cost of change
  reinforced, 43–44
  status quo bias and, 7, 9–10
  with status quo bias defeated, 18
  with status quo bias reinforced, 23
persuadability, in loss frame, myth of
    emotionless executive and, 15f
Peterson, Erik, 5, 122
photography, stock, 151
picture superiority effect, 146–147, 150
pitch
  provocative Why Change, 37
  status quo reinforcement, 36–37
  upsell with provocative, 37
planners
  Why Evolve, 211f
  Why Stay, 204f

positive attitude, boost in, 39
PowerPoint slide, 151
preference stability
  destabilizing, 17–18
  reinforced, 40–42
  status quo bias and, 7, 8–9
  status quo bias reinforced with, 23
pressure, evolving, 172–173
Pre-Suasion (Cialdini), 61
price increase. See also Why Pay
    More conversation
  B2B organization and, 47, 51
  with communication as accidental
    instead of purposeful, 52–53,
    53f
  companies and approaches taken
    for, 53–56, 54f
  with confidence, question of,
    48–50, 49f, 50f
  costs lowered to offset, 54
  as crucial to growth, 47
  customer views on, 49f
  external costs as reason for, 55
  with insight introduced, 55
  justified through better results and
    higher returns, 55
  as must-win commercial moment,
    xx, 3
  with status quo bias reinforced, 55
  structural flaw, 50–52
  timed discount to anchor, 55
price increase conversation
  with anchoring effect, 60–61
  confidence with, 57
  with discount, time-sensitive, 59
  with external cost factors, 60
  with pricing anchor and improved
    capabilities, 58–59
  without pricing anchor and
    improved capabilities, 59

results, 60, 63–64, 62*f*–63*f*

status quo bias reinforcement and, 60

unconsidered need and, 58

Why Pay More condition, 65–68, 65*f*

pricing anchor, 58–61

primacy effect, 113

problem, apology with explanation of, 96

processing
item, 205, 207, 208
services, 205

product as hero, 75–76, 81, 126

productivity
business unit and, 137
IP and, 201
reduced, 166
salesperson, 196, 202

profitability, retention boosting, 30

progress, Why Evolve and, 149

project level, with expansion seller, 137

proof demonstrated, status quo bias defeated with, 19

prospect theory, gain frame and, 18, 84, 165

"provocation-based selling," 6

provocative pitch with upsell, 37

provocative Why Change pitch, 37

The Psychology of Doing Nothing (Anderson), 7–8

purchase intent, 73

Q

question
of confidence and price increase, 48–50, 49*f*, 50*f*
"Why Change," 7
Why Evolve conversation with five, 72–73

R

range of reason, Why Pay More conversation and, 168–169

reality, Why Evolve and, 150

recency effect, 113, 114

regret
anticipated regret and blame, 8, 10–11, 23–24, 43
apology with expression of, 96, 112–113

relationship, stability of, 127, 133

relationship reinforcement and emotion
hard truths shared with, 83–84, 173–174
hybrid, 76, 77*f*, 78*f*–80*f*, 82–87, 82*f*, 86*f*
with pressures highlighted, 83
with results documented, 82–83
with risk of no change emphasized, 84–85
upside opportunity and, 85

renewal. *See also* Why Stay
Corporate Visions survey and, 29*f*, 31*f*, 33*f*
intentions for, 38–39, 38*f*
as must-win commercial moment, xx, 3
with status quo bias reinforced, 38–40
"Why Stay Renewal Study," 35–37

renewal message, 40, 52
customer acquisition and, 30, 33*f*
incumbent advantage and, 31*f*, 32
no clear ownership of, 30–32, 31*f*
unconsidered need and, 64
Why Change and, 63*f*

repair, apology with offer of, 96, 111–112

repentance, apology with declaration
of, 96, 112
response speed, SRP and, 94
responsibility, apology and
acknowledgment of, 96, 112
retention
customer, 91, 131–132, 145
drop in, 145
employee rates for, 36, 41, 58, 65, 67
expansion messaging and
underinvesting in, 29–30, 29f
goals, 43, 66, 70
message and status quo bias,
23–24, 65
profitability boost with, 30
relationship stability and, 127, 133
visual storytelling and, 159
retirement plan, for employees,
36–37, 41, 44
revenue
with apology, 91–92
generating, 30, 127
goals with upsell, 70, 70f
growth, 82, 122, 137, 197
Riesterer, Tim, 5, 122
risk aversion, brain and, 11
risk of change
gain frame and, 13f
mentioned in Why Stay
conversation, 162–164
Why Evolve conversation with no,
174–175
in Why Pay More conversation, 66
in Why Stay message, 43
risk of no change, 84–85, 174–175

S

sale, 5, 122
add-on, 29f, 70f
expansion, 89–97, 145–158, 152f

InsideSales.com, 152
International Journal of Sales
Transformation, 153
"virtual" sales meeting, 153–155
salesperson
with all available items sold to
customer, 179
with belief customers unwilling
to buy new while under
contract, 180
productivity, 196, 202
satisfaction scores, employee, 41, 65
science
apology, 89–97
brain, 3, 12
Decision Science, 5, 6, 21, 113
self-relevance and invoking
imagination, 156
of "sorry," 113–114
selection difficulty
reinforced, 44–45
status quo bias and, 7, 10
with status quo bias reinforced,
23
self-relevance, invoking imagination
and, 156
seller. *See* expansion seller
seller, as mentor, 156–157
selling
all available items to customer,
179
cross-, 130
"provocation-based," 6
Why Change and, 130
Why Evolve and, 130
Why Stay and, 130
service failure scenario
apology components and, 101–104,
103f, 104f
B2B organization and, 104

service failure scenario (*continued*)
  negative emotions with, 100–101
  situational fluency and, 132–134
  test of, 99–100
Service Recovery Paradox (SRP)
  apology and, 90*f*, 94–95, 104, 114
  compensation and, 95
  example of, 90–91
  initiation and, 94
  response speed and, 94
simplicity, with infographics, 148
situational fluency, 191
  piloting, 121–122
  with service failure and apology,
    132–134
  status quo bias and, 122–125
  story, 205–209
  with upsell failure and next steps,
    131–132
  Why Evolve conversation and,
    125–127
  with Why Evolve or Why Change,
    128–129, 130
  with Why Stay or Why Evolve, 128
Smith, Conrad, 5
social influence, Why Evolve message
  framework and, 76
solar system, Copernicus and, 193
"sorry." *See also* apology
  science of, 113–114
  in workplace, 132
  zone of indifference and, 133
SRP. *See* Service Recovery Paradox
stability
  preference, 7, 8–9, 17–18, 23,
    40–42
  of relationship, 127, 133
status quo bias
  with anticipated regret and blame,
    8, 10–11

  with different stories and skills in
    context, 7*f*
  disrupting or defending, 6–16
  with disruption prevention, 21–24
  with emotionless executive, myth
    of, 11–16
  with people chained to current
    state, 8*f*
  perceived cost of change and, 7,
    9–10
  preference stability and, 7, 8–9
  retention message and, 23–24, 65
  selection difficulty and, 7, 10
  situational fluency and, 122–125
status quo bias, defeating
  "acquisition" conversations and, 17*f*
  with contrasting alternative, 18–19
  with costs unchanged, 18
  with current preferences
    destabilized, 17–18
  with proof demonstrated, before
    and after, 19
  Why Change story and, 16,
    19–20, 20*f*
status quo bias, reinforcement of
  with anticipated regret and blame,
    23–24
  customers sticking with current
    solution and, 86*f*
  with "expansion" conversations,
    22*f*
  with perceived cost of change, 23
  with preference stability, 23
  price increase with, 55
  with renewal, intentions for,
    38–39, 38*f*
  renewal with, 38–40
  with selection difficulty, 23
  switching likelihood and, 40, 40*f*
  Why Stay message and, 41*f*

status quo reinforcement pitch,
    "Why Stay Renewal Study" and,
    36–37
stay. *See* Why Stay
stock photography, 151
stories
    contrast with customer, 142–145
    situational fluency, 205–209
    visual storytelling, 145–155, 159
    Why Change, 16, 19–20, 20*f*
subconscious thinking, 11
"sunk cost," 27–28, 27*f*
suppliers, with apology and
    credibility, 109*f*–111*f*
"sure bet," power of incumbency as, 28*f*
"sweet spot," customers in, 26
switching likelihood, 40, 40*f*

T

technology start-ups, 206
thinking
    of customers, 148
    subconscious, 11
The Three Value Conversations
    (Peterson, Riesterer, Smith and
    Geoffrion), 5
time, value over, 26, 26*f*
Tormala, Zakary, 6, 12, 36, 150–151
Triple Metric, 137–139, 138*f*, 160,
    188
truths, hard, 83–84, 173–174
turnover, employee, 84

U

uncertainty, 8–9, 27, 60–61
unconsidered need
    competitive advances and, 45
    insight and, 55
    with preference stability
        destabilized, 17

price increase conversations and,
    58
renewal message and, 64
Why Change and, 62
upsell. *See also* Why Evolve
    Corporate Visions survey and, 70
    cross-sell and, 130
    failure and next steps, 131–132
    as must-win commercial moment,
        xx, 3
    provocative pitch with, 37
    revenue goals with, 70, 70*f*
upside opportunity, 85, 175

V

value, 5
    delivering, 126
    over time, 26, 26*f*
value-based conversation, with
    customer relationship, 190*f*
"vendor-as-hero" language, 157
"virtual" sales meeting, 153–155
visual storytelling
    Corporate Visions survey and,
        150–151
    for expansion sale, 145–155
    painting picture for customers,
        147–148
    retention and, 159
    "virtual" sales meetings and,
        153–155
    Why Evolve, 149–150
void
    with competitors in absence of
        messaging, 181*f*
    with expansion messaging as
        commercial strategy, 189–190,
        190*f*
    messaging, 180–184, 180*f*, 186, 190
Voltaire, 150

W

"we-phrasing," for customer, 157

whole screen image, 151

Why Change. *See also* status quo bias
  provocative pitch with, 37
  question, 7
  relationship reinforcement and
    emotion and, 76, 77f, 78f–80f,
    82–87, 82f, 86f
  renewal message and, 63f
  selling and, 130
  situational fluency with, 128–129,
    130
  with status quo bias, defeating,
    16–21
  story, 16, 19–20, 20f
  unconsidered needs and, 62
  Why Evolve message framework
    and, 76

Why Evolve
  change and, 149
  opportunity and, 150
  progress and, 149
  reality and, 150
  selling and, 130
  situational fluency with, 128–129,
    130
  upsell and, xx, 3, 37, 70, 70f,
    130–132
  visual storytelling, 149–150

Why Evolve conversation
  add-on sales and, 70f
  conversion rates after, 71f
  with customer success, 72
  five questions for, 72–73
  goal of, 3
  hard truths shared in, 83–84,
    173–174
  to incite change, 73
  navigating, 170–175

as personally convincing, 73
to pique interest, 72
pressures highlighted in, 172–173
purchase intent driven by, 73
reasons for, 69
with results documented, 172
risk of no change emphasized in,
  174–175
situational fluency and, 125–127
upside opportunity described in, 175

Why Evolve message framework
  financial services, 205–209
  hybrid, 76, 77f, 82–87, 82f, 86f
  incumbent advantage and, 87, 129
  introduced within contract, 184f
  product as hero and, 75–76
  results, 77–81, 77f, 78f–80f
  social influence and, 76
  Why Change and, 76
  Why Stay and, 76

Why Evolve Planner, 211f

Why Forgive
  apology and, xx, 3, 89–97, 90f,
    92f, 93f, 102, 104, 112–115,
    132–134
  science of "sorry" and, 113–114
  service failure scenario and,
    99–104, 103f, 104f
  winning, 104–111
  winning example, 111–113
  zone of indifference and, 133

Why Pay More conversation, 3, 89
  competitive advances in, 66–67
  cost of change, 66
  decision process reviewed in, 66
  document results of, 65
  message model, 65f
  navigating, 167–170, 170f
  with price increase anchored and
    discount justified, 67

price increase and, xx, 3, 47–68,
  49f, 50f, 53f, 54f, 62f–63f, 65f
range of reason and, 168–169
risk of change in, 66
Why Stay conversation
  with competitive advances
    detailed, 166–167
  with cost of change highlighted,
    164, 166
  with decision process, review of
    prior, 161–162
  moving away from loss and toward
    gain with, 165f
  renewal and, xx, 3, 29f, 30–32, 31f,
    33f, 35–40, 38f, 52, 63f, 64
  with results documented, 160–161
  with risk of change mentioned,
    162–164
Why Stay message
  competitive advances in, 44–45
  Corporate Visions, 196–203
  decision process reviewed in, 42
  document results of, 40–42, 41f,
    123–124
  perceived cost of change in, 43–44
  relationship reinforcement and
    emotion and, 76, 77f, 78f–80f,
    82–87, 82f, 86f

renewal and components of,
  40–45, 41f
risk of change in, 43
selling and, 130
situational fluency with, 128
Why Evolve message framework
  and, 76
Why Stay Planner, 204f
"Why Stay Renewal Study"
  incumbent advantage and, 35–37
  provocative pitch with upsell and, 37
  provocative Why Change pitch
    and, 37
  status quo reinforcement pitch
    and, 36–37
workplace
  employees in, 12–16, 36–37, 41,
    44, 58, 65, 67, 84, 100, 111,
    113, 137
  layoff, 12–16
  "sorry" in, 132

Y

"you-phrasing," with customers,
  155–159, 175

Z

zone of indifference, 99, 133

About the Authors

Erik Peterson
Chief Executive Officer, Corporate Visions, Inc.

Erik has devoted his life's work to improving human communication through science by studying the evidence-based impact of different communication strategies on sales and the selling process. Years ago, Erik earned the nickname "the Professor" because he reached far beyond traditional sales and marketing surveys to apply behavioral research and insights from other disciplines to the results-based world of complex sales.

As the CEO of Corporate Visions, Erik leads a consulting practice of more than 100 consulting professionals who deliver Corporate Visions' work in more than 50 countries. He is also the coauthor of *Conversations That Win the Complex Sale* and *The Three Value Conversations*. His driving passion is to push people and organizations to a place beyond what they believe is possible, because remarkable work is the only kind of work worth doing.

Tim Riesterer

Chief Strategy Officer, Corporate Visions, Inc.

Tim Riesterer has dedicated his career to improving the conversations companies have with prospects and customers. He's previously cowritten three books on the subject—*Customer Message Management, Conversations That Win the Complex Sale,* and *The Three Value Conversations*—based on actual decision-making science research. Tim is a highly sought-after researcher, author, speaker, and consultant in the area of creating and delivering winning customer conversations.

Nick Lee, HLMAM FHEA FAPS

Professor of Marketing, Warwick Business School

Nick Lee received his PhD from Aston University (UK) in 2003. He is currently Professor of Marketing at Warwick Business School. His research interests include sales management, social psychology, cognitive neuroscience, research methodology, and philosophy of science. Nick was editor of the *European Journal of Marketing* from 2008 to 2018 and is currently the incoming editor in chief of the *Journal of Personal Selling and Sales Management.* Nick is an Honorary Fellow of the Association of Professional Sales, which honored him in 2016 for Outstanding Contribution to the Sales Profession. He also holds strategic advisor positions for a number of innovative sales and leadership development companies.

In 2009, Nick was one of the youngest scholars in marketing ever to be appointed to a full professorship, a year in which he was also featured in the *London Times* as "one of the 15 scientists whose work will shape the future." In 2017, he was awarded an Honorary Life Membership of the Academy of Marketing for outstanding lifetime achievements in marketing research. His research has won multiple awards, including the 2018 James M. Comer Award for the Best Contribution to Selling and Sales Management Theory from the *Journal of Personal Selling and Sales Management*, the 2014 Darden Award for Best Methodology Paper from the Academy of Marketing Science, the 2010 Joseph Lister Award Lecture for Social Science from the British Science Association, the 2005 Emerald Outstanding Special Issue Award, and the 2002 EMAC award for best doctoral work. Nick has published over 80 articles since 2005 in journals such as *Organizational Research Methods, Organization Science,* the *Journal of Management, Human Relations,* the *Journal of the Academy of Marketing Science,* the *Journal of Business Ethics, Frontiers in Human Neuroscience,* and the *American Journal of Bioethics,* receiving over 6,200 citations to date. His work has also been featured in the *Financial Times, Forbes, BBC Radio 4, BBC Radio 5Live,* and *BBC Breakfast* and *Al Jazeera* television. His first book, *Doing Business Research,* was published by Sage in 2008, and his book *Business Statistics Using Excel and SPSS* was published by Sage in 2015.

Rob Perrilleon

Senior Vice President, Delivery Services,
Corporate Visions, Inc.

For over 20 years, Rob has developed and implemented effective go-to-market strategies across a range of industries. Today, he combines this knowledge and experience with his passion for marketing and selling success, to lead CVI's global delivery organization. In that role, Rob looks after the messaging consulting, skills training, and content development teams, helping CVI clients find and tell their best story.

Joe Collins

Facilitating Consultant, Corporate Visions, Inc.

With a lifetime fascination for human motivation, Joe earned his bachelor degree in Psychology and an MBA in Global Business Management. He is a firm believer in and proven practitioner of Create Value Skills principles. Joe joined forces with Corporate Visions as a consultant to help you develop impactful stories and ensure your sales team is delivering your company's message with power and passion.

Doug Hutton

Vice President, Training Services, Corporate Visions, Inc.

Doug combines his capability as a trusted advisor to sales and marketing leaders with his leadership of global delivery teams to produce exceptional client learning experiences. At

Corporate Visions, Doug leads an exceptional global team of consultants that enable sellers to create, elevate, capture, and expand value throughout the complex sale, by bringing CVI's decision sciences to life in the classroom. Doug earned his BA from Wake Forest University and MA from The George Washington University.

Leslie Talbot

Vice President, Customer and Commercial Excellence, Corporate Visions, Inc.

A natural storyteller with an engaging style and an abiding love of the written word, Leslie has been crafting and delivering compelling customer conversations for more than 20 years. At Corporate Visions, Leslie helps shape consulting strategy and oversees the application of CVI's intellectual property across every facet of the company's customer and commercial activities.